THE
PERFECTLY
PRODUCTIVE
DAY

THE
PERFECTLY
PRODUCTIVE
DAY

A STEP-BY-STEP GUIDE TO DESIGNING DAYS THAT WORK FOR YOU

SARAH TETLOW

Printed in the United States of America.

For more information or to book a workshop, training, retreat, or event, contact :

hello@perfectlyproductiveday.com
https:/www.firm-focus.com

Book design by Honeylette Pino
Cover design by Tri Widyatmaka

ISBN Paperback: 979-8-9948450-1-1
ISBN Hardcover: 979-8-9948450-0-4
ISBN Kindle: 979-8-9948450-2-8

First Edition: March 2026

CONTENTS

"What got you here won't get you there."
- Marshall Goldsmith

INTRODUCTION

"Perfectly Perfect." That is what Martha Stewart is all about. It is her theme, her motto, if you will. I learned this while I was engulfed in her documentary on Netflix, even though I should have been going to bed.

The thing is, Martha was not perfectly perfect. When you pull back the curtain and catch a glimpse of what her life was really like, you see that while it appeared Perfectly Perfect in many ways, in just as many ways it was not perfect at all.

That is interesting on its own, and it is directly relevant to the book you are about to embark on. What looks Perfectly Perfect is not always the case.

I know what you are thinking, because I know you. You picked up this book because you are exhausted, overwhelmed, and stressed out, and you are searching for the secret sauce to living the Perfectly Perfect Day.

I do not want to burst your bubble on the first page, but that is not exactly what we are talking about here. Perfectly Perfect Days can happen, but they are few and far between, and it usually shows up on vacation, not in the middle of everyday life.

Before we take this journey together into the Perfectly Productive Day, I want to share where the idea for this book came from.

One morning, I was in the shower, which is where I do some of my best thinking. You probably do too, and you will learn more about that when we talk about the Perfectly Productive Morning. That morning, I felt proud of myself for getting up and going to the gym. I did not want to go that day, but despite the resistance, I took each small step to get ready, walked out the door, and headed to the gym before the sun came up.

At this point, back in the shower after my workout, I was riding a euphoric high. I already felt accomplished, motivated, and productive, and my entire family was still asleep. It was at that quiet moment that the idea for this book came to me.

The Perfectly Productive Day.

There are activities you and I do regularly that help us make healthier decisions and take better actions as the day goes on. This is called cognitive priming. It is the idea that what you do early in the day can prime your brain for productivity and positivity. In essence, it sets the stage for a Perfectly Productive Day.

And yet, we are human. There are days when you and I choose, for any number of reasons, not to engage in those habits, even though we know it will affect our mood, energy, and productivity. We end up unproductive and easily distracted because it feels like we have already failed ourselves for the day, so why change now?

Does this resonate with you?

On the journey we are about to take together, we are talking about creating your Perfectly Productive Day. Not a perfect day, but your perfectly productive day.

A Perfectly **Perfect** Day is the kind of day I would love to experience on a trip to Tuscany, surrounded by historical villas, rows and rows of vineyards, and not a stress in the world. Just perfectly perfect.

A Perfectly **Productive** Day is what you can design and live on most typical workdays. The days you spill coffee on your slacks. The days you're conflicted between too many priorities at work. The days that you squeeze in homework help, sports practice, dinner, and baths all in one night. The days you skip the gym in the morning, but still have the ability to take control and make the rest of the day rock.

A Perfectly Productive Day is about building habits that work for you, prioritizing self-care, and focusing on what truly has to get done, rather than letting outside noise hijack your best intentions.

Did you know there are simple tools, habits, and strategies that have been proven to set you up for a Perfectly Productive Day?

They are so simple that you can learn and implement them today. They work as small, one percent changes, and they can create a significant impact.

The Perfectly Productive Day that you and I will customize together is grounded in science and research around what is healthy, what optimizes you, and what truly supports productivity. It is built on routines and habits I use on my most productive days, and on what others, like you, have discovered they need to set themselves up for a Perfectly Productive Day.

Before we go any further, I want you to know something important.

We probably have more in common than you realize.

- Are you a hardworking professional who is deeply committed to your career or business?
- Do you have a never-ending To-Do list that seems to grow by the minute?
- Do you get easily distracted, overwhelmed, and stressed by everything that needs to get done? It often feels like there is too much to do and not enough time to do it.

- Are you a busy, middle-aged woman who works outside the home and also serves as the CEO of your household, with everything that role includes? (And if you're a man reading this, stay with us – the strategies and tools in this book will also apply to you.)

If the above statements resonate with you, then you and I are a lot alike, and we understand each other. Every one of those statements describes me on most days. And yet, many days I am a productive superstar. Even in chaos, I know that you are a productivity powerhouse too. If you do not fully believe that yet, you will by the time we finish this book together.

This work is not theoretical for me. It is personal. I spend my days studying productivity, building strategies, and helping people create days that actually work in real life. What I have learned, over and over again, is that productivity is not about perfection. It is about understanding yourself and building habits that support you, even on messy, imperfect days.

Up until today, you may have been waiting for the perfect moment to change your behavior. That moment is now. Even with everything you have going on, this book found you at exactly the right time in your life, when you are ready to receive it.

In *The Alchemist* by Paulo Coelho, the king says, "When you want something, all the universe conspires in helping you to achieve it." That is what happened when you picked up this book. You are exactly where you are meant to be to create and live your Perfectly Productive Day, and you will reap the rewards of more time, more money, and far less overwhelm.

You and I both live full, hectic lives, and we share a desire to make a difference, not only in the world around us but in our lives as well. We are both trying to find that elusive balance between showing up for others and making space for ourselves.

We lead lives filled to the brim with work, family, friends, and all the responsibilities that come with adulthood. Yet we're determined to be our most productive selves, constantly seeking ways to optimize our time and energy.

With that reality in mind, this book is organized around the natural rhythm of a workday, Monday through Friday, for most of us. You can think of each day as unfolding through six core categories, with the commute acting as the bookends that carry us into and out of the workday.

Those categories are:

1. Morning Routine
2. Commute (before and after the workday)
3. Workday
4. Evening Routine
5. Bedtime Routine
6. Sleep Routine

The book is broken down this way so you can focus on one small part of your day at a time. Real change rarely comes from overhauling everything at once. It comes from small, intentional shifts that build on each other. When those small changes are repeated and compounded, they quietly reshape the entire day.

Within each category, you will find chapters that explore the most important elements of that part of the day. Our exploration will start with a story, then we will go into strategies backed by research and science to show proven paths to building your Perfectly Productive Day.

And because I am human, I will also share the bloopers. The moments when I know what works, yet still manage to drift off track. You will recognize these moments because they happen to you, too. Together, we will look at what went sideways and how to approach it differently next time.

If at any point you feel a little nervous, like this might be more than you can handle, pause right there. You are not taking on everything at once. You are simply making one small adjustment at a time.

Productivity Isn't One-Size-Fits-All

Recently, I coached Emily, a litigation attorney navigating long workdays while raising two young children on her own. She reached out because she felt like she was living on a hamster wheel, constantly moving and barely staying upright.

Emily told me she felt alone. Everywhere she looked, her colleagues seemed to have it all together. Deadlines were met. Targets were hit. Kids' activities were attended. From the outside, it looked effortless.

She felt especially discouraged when she compared her day-to-day reality with coworkers, friends, and the carefully curated lives she saw on social media and television. It seemed as though everyone else had discovered a secret she somehow missed.

Most of us have felt this way at some point. Comparison has a way of distorting reality, especially when we are measuring our lives against carefully selected snapshots.

Take the color-coordinated homes on organizing shows. What looks like a perfectly ordered life is often a fleeting moment staged for a camera. Real life resumes the second the crew packs up. Kids pull supplies back out. Cabinets get marked up again. Order, like productivity, is rarely permanent. This is the reason most productivity approaches fail. They lack flexibility and adaptability. When a system is too rigid, it is bound to break.

Or consider the polished, confident twenty-something dominating your Instagram feed. Her primary responsibility may be her online presence, not a household, a demanding career, or caregiving responsibilities layered on top of each other.

The same goes for the professional traveling the world on a book tour. Writing and speaking are his full-time focus. He is not balancing the same constraints, competing priorities, or invisible labor that many professionals carry.

This is why productivity is not about perfection. It is about progress.

It is about making small, intentional changes that support what you actually need, not what looks impressive from the outside. It is about choosing habits and routines that move you toward growth, fulfillment, and a sense of accomplishment that feels true at the end of the day.

I created my company, Firm Focus, to help high-performing professionals regain control of their time, energy, and daily workload. Originally designed for attorneys, it focuses on streamlining workflows and intentionally preparing for each workday, so work feels proactive rather than constantly reactive.

One of our coaches, Debbie Rosemont, captures this idea beautifully. She defines productivity as **achieving desired results**.

She begins each day by identifying the result she wants to achieve, then evaluates whether her plans, tasks, and commitments will support that outcome. Productivity is measured not by activity, but by alignment.

If the desired result is rest and recovery, a day that includes a nap, a gentle walk, and meaningful connection is a productive day. It may not look impressive to an outsider, but it delivers exactly what is needed.

As we begin this journey together, I want to be clear about how to use what follows. I will share the habits, behaviors, and actions that shape my perfectly productive day. These examples are meant to demonstrate what is possible, not to prescribe a rigid formula.

Your work is to experiment. To test what fits your life, your responsibilities, and your priorities. To keep what helps you be the productive version of yourself that you want to be and to discard what does not. The goal is to build a version of productivity that actually supports you.

You are not stuck, and you are not alone – as Emily described feeling. One of the quiet privileges of adulthood is the ability to choose change on purpose. If where you are right now is no longer working, you can move, and you can grow. You are someone who lives with a growth mindset, which is why you are reading this book. You were never meant to live in a constant state of overwhelm, and your life is not ruled by fate.

This is your opportunity to feel more in control, more productive, and more fulfilled.

You can do this. There is nothing that can stand in your way.

Limiting Beliefs and Negative Self-Talk

As you begin reading this book, you may notice something that feels as though it is standing in your way. You may have moments when you compare yourself to others and immediately turn that comparison inward. You may experience thoughts like:

"I will never be organized."

"I feel so behind."

"I'll never be productive."

"I am a failure."

"This is just the way it has to be."

Those thoughts are common, but they are also signs of a fixed mindset, and they are not true.

Humans are wired to scan for what might go wrong. That instinct once kept our ancestors alive. Today, it often shows up as automatic negative self-talk. While those thoughts are normal, they are not facts, and you do not have to accept them as truth. Your brain tells convincing stories, but that does not make them accurate.

As you move through this book, I invite you to start removing phrases like "I am not," "I will never," "and "I can't change" from your vocabulary. They no longer serve you.

Angela Duckworth is an American academic and psychologist, and the author of Grit: The Power of Passion and Perseverance. She admitted that she was challenged by her therapist to remove the word "should" from her vocabulary. As in, "I should go to the gym" or "I should work on this report."

While not simple, I've been cognizant of when I insert the word "should" into my day-to-day, and I've been making an effort to remove it. It isn't always easy, but it is impactful and encourages me to pause and consider if that activity is what I need and/or want to do.

When you catch yourself slipping into the pattern of negative self-talk or saying "should" about things, then I encourage you to pause and redirect. Try starting with:

"I can do better."

"I am doing my best."

"I am capable of change."

"I am worthy."

"I am productive."

"I want to do this."

Small shifts in language matter because they shape how you see yourself.

There is a simple reason this works. Self-Perception Theory, introduced by psychologist Daryl Bem, explains that we come to believe who we are by observing how we act. When you begin behaving like an organized and productive person, even in small ways, your identity starts to align with those actions. Behavior leads, belief follows.

Neurosurgeon Dr. James Doty explains that the negative dialogue in our heads is not true, yet we often believe it and let it limit what we think is possible. He says:

"The challenge for so many of us is that we believe the negative self-talk that we have and, as a result, we create limited beliefs that limit our possibilities, and we believe this ongoing narrative.

The reality is that we have more power within ourselves, and it is understanding that we control this. You can't wait for somebody to magically take care of everything. The reality is, you have the power within yourself to change your circumstance, and it is just believing it."

When we repeatedly tell ourselves something cannot be done, that story becomes our reality. The power to change that narrative has always been ours.

Who you believe you are is who you become.

Read that again and let it land.

You may hear encouragement from coaches, books, or even from me as you read these pages. That encouragement matters, but it cannot replace your own belief. Lasting change only happens when you begin to see yourself differently.

As you close this introduction and move into the pages ahead, here is what I want you to imagine. A life where you trust yourself. Where you set intentions and know you can follow through, even on days that get hijacked. A life where productivity no longer feels fragile or dependent on perfect conditions, but grounded in habits you can return to again and again.

That version of you is not hypothetical. It is built one choice, one habit, and one day at a time.

Let's begin with the Perfectly Productive Morning.

Morning Routine

. . . .

CHAPTER 1

Starting the Day Intentionally

The first home my husband, Andy, and I shared was a studio apartment built on top of a garage in Montecito, California. Yes, that Montecito, where Prince Harry and Meghan Markle were married and where Oprah's sprawling estate takes up a shocking amount of land. I'm exaggerating, but not by much.

The setting and landscape of our new home felt special. A quiet street lined with eucalyptus trees. A long gravel driveway leading past a beautiful farmhouse. An unlit path wrapped around the garage and opened up to a white exterior staircase that led to our front door. It felt like a retreat.

Inside, the studio stretched the full length of the large garage below it. With thoughtful furniture placement and a lot of hand-me-downs from my Oma (that's grandma in Dutch), we managed to carve the space into a kitchen, dining area, living room, bedroom, and even a small office nook. It wasn't fancy, but it worked.

There were quirks, of course. The floor was made of tightly woven rope, the kind that looks charming until you walk barefoot on it. Shoes were strongly encouraged.

French doors off the living room opened to a small balcony overlooking the Santa Ynez Mountains. We would step outside, breathe in the crisp mountain air, and take in the quiet. The apartment, the view, the town, it all felt serene, beautiful, and from the outside, perfect.

I'm sharing this detail for one reason. That seemingly perfect apartment had a major flaw. Well, two, if you count the rope floors.

Every single morning, at the butt crack of dawn, the homeowners' rooster crowed. And this was not the polite rooster crow you might be imagining. This rooster was aggressive, erratic, and relentless. We were convinced something was wrong with him.

According to *The Old Farmer's Almanac*, roosters crow to signal safety, establish dominance, and warn of danger. If that's true, then Montecito must have been crawling with threats, because this rooster sounded like it was defending the entire town.

We lived in that apartment for eighteen months. And for all eighteen of those months, my mornings started off on the wrong foot. Because, as science, research, and this book will show, waking up to external disturbances hijacking your sleep is one of the least productive ways to start your day.

It All Begins in the Morning -- Or Does It?

Fast forward to today, Tuesday, April 2, almost twenty years later, I have tested, tried, and adopted the Perfectly Productive Morning (for me). My morning routine today, which I will explain, has been proven by countless researchers, neuroscientists, and doctors.

This is somewhat of a trick, though. You see, establishing the Perfectly Productive Morning Routine is directly connected to Perfectly Productive Sleep.

Seems logical, right? But it continues.

A good night's sleep is contingent on when, how, and where you go to sleep. And when, how, and where you go to sleep is determined by your Perfectly Productive Bedtime Routine, which is related to your Perfectly Productive Evening Routine, which is triggered by how, when, and why you finish your Perfectly Productive Workday.

Are you following me here?

In deciding where and how to start this book, I really struggled. Do you remember learning the song that went:

> *"Your knee bone connected to your…thigh bone.*
> *Your thigh bone connected to your…hip bone.*
> *Your hip bone connected to your…back bone."*

This song, called *Dem Bones*, is a great comparison to this book. Each part is separate but relies heavily on the other parts of the day. A terrible commute can throw you off and lead to an unproductive day at work. An inconsistent bedtime routine can lead to poor sleep, which might affect how you start your day. Creating the Perfectly Productive Day requires that we look at who you are and how you spend your day holistically.

A Perfectly Productive Morning does not necessarily create a Perfectly Productive Day. A Perfectly Productive Morning is only possible if you are bought into the concept of a Perfectly Productive Sleep and a Perfectly Productive Workday.

We will start the book by focusing on the morning, as it seems fitting. Just remember, we will revisit each part of your day as we go through because, like a bike chain, we need every part to do its part, or we will not be able to gain momentum.

Dan Beck is a wealth advisor for HENRYS (High-Earners Not Yet Rich) at Equitable Advisors, and he lives in San Francisco, California. Dan responded to my question, *"What does a Perfectly Productive Day mean to you?"* by stating:

> *"My day starts the night before by going to bed early, generally before 9:00 p.m. I wake up between 5:00 a.m. and 6:00 a.m. to ensure that I get a full eight to nine hours of sleep before I start my day."*

Perfectly said, Dan.

Our Perfectly Productive Day starts the night before, and that leads to the Perfectly Productive Morning.

With that in mind, here is my Perfectly Productive Morning.

The Way to Start the Day

I remember when my great-aunt bought me a digital radio alarm clock when I turned twelve. It was just after an ice-skating competition, and I was ecstatic when I opened it. I'm guessing because it had a radio component to it, a novelty at my age.

To this day, I still use that alarm clock to wake up, albeit the choice of waking music has likely changed dramatically since the early 1990's.

After turning off the alarm (yes, turning **off** the alarm and not by hitting snooze), my initial thought is almost always, "noooooo...I want to go back to sleep. I want to find out what happened to that two-headed snake who was talking to the sleep monkey's cousin in the purple skylight."

I have weird dreams. Don't judge me.

I lay there for a minute or so, inviting my conscious mind to come to life. Now, at this point, I am still almost always battling the choice to just roll over and go back to sleep. And sometimes I do, which will be covered later in the Perfectly Unproductive Morning. But, on my Perfectly Productive Days, after lying for a minute or two, I say in my head "five, four, three, two ... one," and I kick off the sheets and comforter and spring out of bed.

My husband is still soundly sleeping (no, really, you'd hear it if you were here), and so I smooth over and make my side of the bed.

I've already dropped a few clues here about the Perfectly Productive Morning. One of those clues is to make my bed. Andy, my husband, contributed to my crowdsourcing question with what helps him have a Perfectly Productive Day by sharing that:

> *"Every morning when I wake up, I fully make the bed—decorative pillows and all. This habit sets me up to retain organization throughout the day, and my wife says that seeing the bed made reminds her that our bedroom is a calm and controlled space."*

I've taught him well.

Since Andy is still asleep when I get up, making the bed is probably a more accurate representation of what I do each morning. Not exactly making the bed, but the habit of folding the sheets and comforter over and running my hand over them to smooth them out is a small signal that represents control and order in my day.

My side of the bed is made, and I'm up on my own two feet. I grab my phone and my book and walk into our bathroom.

And yes, I'll admit it: my phone sits right next to me on the nightstand when I sleep. Not exactly what the experts recommend. Most sleep specialists strongly advise keeping your phone out of reach at night.

And honestly, they have a point.

It's not just because phones are distracting. It's because they compete for your attention the second you open your eyes. And once they have it, they can hijack your morning… and even the benefits of a perfectly productive night's sleep.

Does any of this sound familiar?

You wake up at night and check emails, scroll social media, watch a show, or play games. Or you rely on your phone to wake you up in the morning. Or you are watching it as you fall asleep. Or you struggle with waking up in the morning, and you chronically turn off the alarm (on your phone) and fall back to sleep.

Each of these common behaviors is why the experts recommend that you leave your phone in another room, which will help mitigate these unproductive and unhealthy habits. People who know they are likely to grab their phone in the night build systems to keep it away instead of relying on willpower.

Tony Quintong lives in the East Bay outside of San Francisco, and he is a Chief Executive Officer for companies on a fractional basis. Tony Q., or Q as we often call him, said that his Perfectly Productive Day starts with affirmations in the evening (there is that theme again – our Perfectly Productive Day starts the night before). He also said:

> *"I shut my phone off (the night before) and place it somewhere farthest from the bedroom. Truth be told, my two adult children and their families live far from me and my wife, Renee. Our son lives in Nairobi, Kenya, and our daughter lives*

in Miami, Florida. They know the importance of keeping us updated; however, they respect our time zones. If they text 411, it means call within a few hours and let us know, nothing urgent. However, if they text 911, they need an immediate call."

Establishing some boundaries is helpful and critical for setting up his Perfectly Productive Morning. Note, however, that as part of those boundaries, Tony has created a gate and an access code for entry. When his children message 911 before their text, Q and Renee understand that their immediate response is needed. A 411 text honors their schedule and requests a response at their convenience. In addition, the beautiful thing about technology these days is that you can create an override on your phone to ring when the 911 texts come through (and remain silent when a lower-priority communication is received).

Anne Sharp, a Certified Professional Organizer (CPO®) and owner of A Sharp Space in Boston, Massachusetts, knows herself well. She says she leaves her cell phone in the kitchen overnight so she isn't tempted to check it in the middle of the night. Even as an organizer, she sometimes struggles with the pull of the cell phone.

Sahiba Bassi noticed that checking her phone first thing in the morning immediately put her into reactive mode, so she now uses tools like app limits and scheduled access to social media.

Relying on willpower alone is never enough. You need tools and systems. In my presentations and client work, I often return to this idea: productive people use tools and systems to stay **on track**. We will return to this when we come full circle in the Perfectly Productive Bedtime Routine.

For now, let's keep moving.

By the time I reach the bathroom, it is about 4:30 a.m., and I am still sluggish and half asleep. You know the feeling, eyes barely open, mouth not quite closed, feet moving slower than they were designed to. I set my book and phone on the counter and flip on the light above the shower, just enough to brighten the room without putting a spotlight directly over my head.

After using the restroom, I walk over to a small round bench where a neat pile of clothes awaits me. This is not accidental. That pile is a gift from my Perfectly Productive Evening Routine Self to my Perfectly Productive Morning Routine Self, a quiet nudge to follow through on the commitment I made the night before to get to the gym. I am always thinking about my Future Self and what she will need to succeed.

That idea is at the heart of Be Your Future Self Now by Benjamin Hardy. He argues that long-term success comes from living in alignment with the person you are becoming. When your future self is clear, your present-day decisions gain direction. You avoid unnecessary friction, reduce distractions, and stay motivated because your environment is already supporting the outcome you want.

This is an important step, according to the experts, for ensuring you reach your goals and develop habits: consider the future version of yourself and what that person looks like, and the actions that they take.

Laura Doehle is an organizational efficiency expert and owner of Elevation Business Consulting, based just outside of Seattle, Washington. Supporting the theme that we have established so far in the Perfectly Productive Morning, Laura says:

> *"I stop looking at my phone before I go to bed; it stays downstairs. I walk the dogs first thing (in the morning and) before I check my phone (which I take on the walk for safety but without ever*

looking at it). If I'm going to work out, I do that without looking at my phone. Not until I'm done with this ritual will I glance through my phone. I find that if I look too soon, my brain focuses on the wrong things while working out."

You've done that before, right?

We all have. We all have had the situation where we read an email, text, or social media post that hijacks our thoughts and mindset. We may have just had the most peaceful sleep ever, and now we are noodling over someone else's input on something (or maybe even fuming over it).

This episode touches on something we will be talking more about later. This displays why multitasking is often frowned upon when you are actually trying to get stuff done. We'll dive into it a lot more during The Perfectly Productive Workday.

Back to my morning in the bathroom and staring at the small gift from my Perfectly Productive Evening Routine self. The pile is waiting, ready for me to step into it and encouraging me to follow through on the commitment I made the night before.

And, at the same time, I am human, and I struggle just like you do. At this point, I am still having a silent, solo debate in my head. I am not a magical fairy person who can decide to wake up at 4:30 a.m. to go to the gym, and the movements that follow are as easy as the decision to have an ice cream sundae with hot fudge, nuts, whipped cream, and three cherries, and that contains zero calories to boot.

Nope. I am battling every second of this. I want to go back to sleep. I want to crawl into my cozy bed and fall back into dreamland. This is never easy, not even for those of us who have mastered the Perfectly Productive Morning.

For you and me alike, when the alarm goes off in the morning, there is a moment in time where we both hesitate. You *think* about what you need to do instead of *doing* it. Do you understand the difference?

When we *think* about what we need to do, we often take the steps towards easy, comfortable, and often unproductive action.

When we **do** what we need to do, we often take the harder, less comfortable, and (ironically) more productive actions.

It is unmistakable when you experience this brief moment of hesitation. It is a habit, and we all do it.

One of my favorite people on the planet is motivational speaker, Mel Robbins. We are best friends – although she doesn't know it because we haven't met each other yet. Mel is the world's leading expert on motivation, habits, and change.

Mel calls this brief moment in time "the five-second moment of hesitation," and it is that moment where you start *thinking* about doing something, instead of **doing** it. Those five seconds will impact your behavior. Instead of thinking about getting out of bed, the healthier habit is to just do it. Get out of bed. Take the next step and progress.

> *"Researchers, psychologists, and neuroscientists explain this five-second window this way: There are two types of people. There are people who have a bias towards thinking, which is the habit of hesitating and thinking about what they need to do instead of doing what they need to do. And then there are people who have a bias towards action. Which is the habit of pushing yourself to take action regardless of how you feel. This five-second countdown helps you move from being a person who has a bias towards **thinking** and become a person who has a bias towards **action**."*

If you recall, when I want to stay in bed and keep on dreaming, when I don't want to wake up, I count down from five and spring out of bed. This is because of the habit developed through Mel's Five-Second Rule.

There are three important things that usually help me **act** in the moment, rather than just thinking about it. **My Three Perfectly Productive Pushes** are:

1. **Building the Habit.**

   Creating the habits of the Perfectly Productive Day and laying out my clothes the night before. This habit applies the Progress Principle -- the idea that small wins build momentum toward bigger goals -- and supports the progress I have already made toward my goal of going to the gym...before I ever wake up!

2. **Accountability.**

   Signing up for a class at my gym, so I will be charged if I don't show up. When I feel like I am about to make the wrong decision and go back to bed, I sign up for the class, which means the gym will charge me a fee if I do not show up. Yikes.

3. **Considering the Future Me.**

   Checking in with myself and auditing it against the person I want to be. In an hour, am I going to be the version of me who went back to sleep? Or am I the version of me who got up and got the Perfectly Productive Morning accomplished!?

Considering and envisioning the Future You is a fascinating, well-researched concept known as Future Self Continuity. This concept bridges psychology, neuroscience, and behavioral economics, and it refers to how strongly a person feels *connected* to their future self — essentially, how much they perceive their future self as the same person as they are today.

Hal Hershfield, a professor at the UCLA Anderson School of Management, and Daniel Gilbert, an American social psychologist, used neuroimaging to show that thinking about your future self activates brain regions similar to those activated when you think about *a stranger*. This means many people treat their future selves almost like another person.

However, the more you invest in trying to view your future self as a *continuation* of your true and present self (rather than a stranger), the more likely you are to make long-term, beneficial decisions — like saving for retirement, eating healthily, or avoiding procrastination.

Behavioral nudges, such as framing choices as helping "your future self," can improve decision-making, like "Your future self will thank you for flossing," or "don't be a jerk to your future self by not finishing this memo now."

Give it a try. What is something that you want the Future You to do? I'd recommend starting small by thinking about something the Future You—just one hour from now—will have done. Write that down in *The Perfectly Productive Day Workbook*, a companion to this book available on the resource page via the QR Code at the end of the book. The workbook is designed to help you complete exercises like this one, go deeper with take-action prompts, and reflect on provoking questions that bring the ideas in these pages to life.

Now, what is something that the Future You in a day will have accomplished? Write that down.

Consider the Future You in one week from now. What is that date? What will you have accomplished? Write that down.

How about the Future You in six months to a year from now? What is she doing that you are not currently doing? Write that down.

I often try to lean on the habits I have developed to consider the Future Sarah Tetlow as a continuation of today's Sarah Tetlow. The habits that help me take action today will benefit me tomorrow. It's not always easy, though.

Given that I am not perfect, and I am human, there are many mornings when I say screw it, and I do fall back to sleep. I'll tell you more about that later. For now, we are staying on the Perfectly Productive Morning.

Ok, we are back in the bathroom on this Perfectly Productive Morning, and we are looking at that little gift from the Perfectly Productive Evening Routine. There sits this pile of workout clothes waiting and ready for me to put them on and do the right thing to set myself up for success today.

Battling that little voice telling me to go back to sleep, I start to go through the pile. I put on the sports bra.

No, Sarah, go back to sleep. It's sooooo cozy and soft and lovely and….

I lift my left foot to slip it into the leggings, then set it back on the warm porcelain tile.

I lift my right leg and try to avoid falling over while I put it through the other leg of my workout pants.

At this point, that voice in my head reminds me that it isn't too late. I could even fall back to sleep with the leggings and sports bra on.

And then that other voice – the future Sarah Tetlow voice – says, "Oh, shut up, you! I'm taking another step towards my Perfectly Productive Morning!" I work hard to avoid *thinking* about what I need to do and instead do it, thanks to **My Three Perfectly Productive Pushes.**

I splash a little body spray onto my skin and put deodorant under my arms. My workout shirt is next on the pile, and I slip my arms through the holes and pull the tank over my head.

The inner me is still having an intense dialogue, trying to convince me to take the comfortable route of crawling back into bed rather than the *productive* route of going to the gym.

I push forward.

My socks and shoes are next, and I put those on. Now, this is a critical point in the morning routine. Because once those socks and shoes are on, I have pretty much told the little Devil in my mind that she lost the battle of sending me back into dreamland. And I really hate to disappoint her because she gets really moody, argumentative, and cranky.

However, when she gets her way, when the little Devil in my head wins, and I go back to sleep, then it usually means she controls my emotions for the rest of the day. So, in this moment, I flick her off of my shoulder, and I continue with tying my laces (often not tight enough because 3 out of 4 times on the treadmill, I have to stop to tie them again. You'd think I'd learn by now.)

The socks and shoes are on my feet, and I am now ready to head to the gym.

Do you remember where I left my cell phone and my book? They are still sitting on the bathroom counter, and I have not lifted either one yet. Which means I have not looked at my phone at all. In fact, you will learn that on my Perfectly Productive Days, I often do not look at my phone until much, much later in the morning.

The last thing left on the round bench by the Perfectly Productive Evening Routine Me is my journal. At this point, I sit on the round bench, and I complete a journal entry for the day. My journal has prompts, but the point is to brain dump what is in your head before you let anything external into your precious mind-space.

Consider how you would answer these **Seven Perfectly Productive Day Primer** questions. Use the Perfectly Productive

Day Workbook, grab a blank sheet of paper, or use lipstick on your mirror and answer:

- *How did you sleep?*
- *How are you really feeling right now?*
- *What do you need to make this a good day?*
- *What will help energize you?*
- *What do you need to get done today?*
- *Why is it important? How can you motivate yourself to get it done?*
- *How will you celebrate when you finish it?*

The idea here is to align with your body, first, on how you're feeling, and also to be clear on what you know you need to do today. Maybe you need to work on a big presentation for your boss. Maybe you want to clean out a closet. Maybe you'd benefit from doing something for yourself today, since you need it and you've prioritized it for this day. (Notice I never said "should" do these things.)

Writing in the journal doesn't need to take more than a minute or two, but its impact is significant.

Is this helpful? Are you following along and imagining what you can do to start living your Perfectly Productive Morning? If so, awesome, I'm glad to have you here with me, and there is so much more to uncover. If not, it's probably your little Devil talking and, as a result, you're just cranky and being argumentative. Tell her to shut up and keep reading; you still have a lot to learn.

You might be thinking, "but I'd have to check my calendar…in my email…on my phone, in order to answer the question about my top priority today." Well, then, I encourage you to read on.

Remember that the Perfectly Productive Day is created by all of its parts (*Dem Bones*), and all of its parts mean that we are going to cover how to end your Perfectly Productive Workday so that you feel empowered and confident about what you have going on the next day. Already knowing, generally, what you have scheduled and what you need to do the next day, you're better able to answer these prompts in your journal.

And since where you stand right now, you haven't yet read the Perfectly Productive Evening Routine, here is what you can do today and this week. Just write down whatever top-priority task or action comes to mind. Doing that will give you clarity about what you're feeling anxious about, because your subconscious brought it forward while you were sleeping. Bring that important To-Do with you when we start our Perfectly Productive Workday.

Alright, I am dressed, I've brain dumped my thoughts, and now I'm ready to walk out the door.

Oh, wait, one more very important step in the morning! No, it isn't looking at my phone! It is grabbing my electric toothbrush with my right hand, pulling off the cap, grabbing the toothpaste from the drawer, and spreading it on the toothbrush. Brushing for two to three minutes (going off the feeling of being clean and not the length of time suggested by four out of five dentists), then I rinse my mouth and the toothbrush, cap it, and I'm ready to head out the door. I pick up my book, my cell phone, and my workout towel and walk out of our bathroom.

Ironically, I have to walk past the bed to leave the house at this point. There's still a chance to give it all up and crawl back in bed. I could just bend down, pull one lace on each shoe, slip them off, and slip into my cozy bed…

No. I'm going.

I've done everything right so far this Perfectly Productive Morning, so why stop now?

At this point, it is typically around 4:45 a.m., and I enter the garage, open the driver's seat of my car, click the garage door opener, and turn on the engine. I'd be lying if I said I am 100% motivated and committed to going to the gym. In fact, there are times that that little she-Devil in my head is still trying to convince me that I could turn around and go back to bed. Yet, most days, I press on, fighting the lack of motivation and instead focusing on the future reward.

Dr. Alok Kanojia is an American psychiatrist and co-founder of Healthy Gamer, a mental health coaching company. Dr. K, as he is often referred to as, is an expert on motivation. He emphasizes that motivation is less about waiting for the perfect feeling and more about intentional action, particularly by leveraging motivational interviewing techniques that help people talk themselves into change rather than being persuaded by external incentives or internal pressure.

His practical theory of motivation blends neuroscience, behavioral change techniques, and environmental structuring. He considers a grounded, accessible approach focused on self-awareness, action, and reclaiming control from overwhelming dopamine triggers. Keeping his research in mind, I propel forward.

In my car, dressed for the gym, and ready to drive the two miles there, I back out of my garage and cruise down the road. Once at the gym, I grab what I need to walk in: my workout gloves, towel, heart rate monitor, purse, water bottle, and whatever book I am currently reading. Yes, I grab a book.

If you're following along, which I imagine you are since you're reading this book, you may have noticed that I still have not looked at my cell phone. That's right. It's with me, in my purse, but I have yet to look at it. Like Laura, I carry it with me for safety, comfort, and habit, but I have not yet looked at it. My goal at the gym is to focus on what is inside my head, not on the frustrating, exciting, or interesting external content that exists in that little digital box.

Once inside the gym, I secure my space in the class, and while waiting for the class to start, I sit down and crack open my book. Sometimes I have a friend taking the class, and we will chat, but most people at the gym know that I enjoy reading before class, and they leave me alone. That, or most people think that I am totally weird and avoid me.

Here's the deal about the reading that I do at the gym in the morning. Every year, I set a goal to read a certain number of books for that year.

In 2019, I set a goal to read nineteen books. In 2020, it was twenty books, and in 2024, when I started writing this book, it was twenty-four books. When you consider that goal, say twenty-four books in 2024, and you break it down, you have a pace at which to finish a book in order to succeed in reaching that goal.

In 2024, it was conveniently equal to two books per month. Well, to read two books per month while owning a business, running a household, going to the gym, and ultimately living a Perfectly Productive Day, I needed to find opportune times to read. The five to twelve minutes in the morning waiting for my workout class to start is one of those times. Besides, it keeps me off my phone, and it also sets the scene for a Perfectly Productive Day.

You, too, are a reader because you are reading this book. Did you pick up this book because someone recommended it, or did you want to be more productive? Or, do you consider yourself a frequent and avid reader? If the former, consider reading more often. Set a goal – even if it is five books a year, or twelve, or fifteen. Or even if you don't want to set a goal, instead just make an effort to choose a book over your little device more often than not.

We've talked a lot about our Future Self, and another advantage of creating a reading goal is that this habit benefits, considers, and enhances the Future Me. What does the Future You look like – someone who knows everything about your high school acquaintances' social media lives? Or someone who is well-read, like Warren Buffett?

Warren Buffett, the billionaire investor and CEO of Berkshire Hathaway, is famously known for spending a significant amount of time in his day reading. While it may appear that he makes important business decisions quickly, Buffett has said that his ability to act decisively is actually the result of hours—often years—of thoughtful reading and reflection.

He doesn't rush decisions; he prepares for them.

His steady habit of reading builds a deep reservoir of insight so that when the moment comes to choose, he's already done the thinking.

It's a powerful reminder that a few quiet moments with a book each morning can serve as mental training for sharper, faster decision-making later in the day.

Finally, breaking up my annual reading goal into smaller and bite-sized actions that I can achieve on a regular basis helps with follow-through on other beneficial behaviors beyond just the reading goal itself.

In his studies, Psychologist Peter Gollwitzer found that people who formed implementation intentions were two to three times more likely to follow through on a task than those who only set general goals. In other words, the clearer and more habitual a morning routine is, for example, the more likely a person is to follow through on productive intentions throughout the day.

The point is that setting a goal and breaking it down helps you prioritize that activity over something meaningless but satisfying in the moment. The same theory can apply to working out and establishing a goal around the frequency with which you do so.

CHAPTER 2

Preparing Your Mind and Body

Now that I am at the gym during my Perfectly Productive Morning and I've checked in at my station, I usually sit on a bench in the lobby and open my book. Some days, I might only read a page or two before my workout class starts. On other days, I can finish a chapter. In a weird way, the whole roulette of how much I am able to read is part of the fun.

The coach calls the start of the class, and at that point, I place my purse and my book into a locker and walk into the studio and find my station.

In case you're wondering, the gym that I work out at is OrangeTheory® Fitness. The reason I love OrangeTheory® Fitness is that it takes the large, overwhelming task of working out for an hour and breaks it down into micro moments. The short blocks, the different sides of the room, the 30-second sprints, or the three-minute runs. It helps me, and others too, I imagine, to look at the workout as these smaller tasks and not the big project of working out for an hour.

The important point here is to try to prioritize moving your body as part of your morning routine. Or at least moving your body before you have allowed other inputs – social media, email, text messages – to enter your mind. This way, your mind prioritizes your needs before considering the needs, demands, and thoughts of others.

I am also not intending to imply that you need to get a full-body workout done in the morning. Doing that works well for me because I prefer to work out in the morning, and it helps me ensure I check that box and get that activity done. The overall point is to move your body in the morning, since there's quite a bit of science supporting the idea that moving your body—even briefly—can significantly improve focus, mood, and productivity throughout the day.

A 2016 review in *Neuropsychopharmacology* showed that physical activity boosts the neurotransmitters in your brain, making you feel more awake and motivated. It results in effects similar to coffee but without the caffeine crash later on. Starting to move your body in the morning, before coffee, may lead to actually drinking less of it throughout the day, which will also help with your overall fatigue.

Dr. Wendy Suzuki is a neuroscientist who studies, amongst other things, neuroplasticity in the brain. Dr. Suzuki explains that she conducted a study on herself while pursuing tenure at New York State. She compares some form of exercise, even a ten-minute walk, to a brain bubble bath. Dr. Suzuki says,

> *"Every single time that you move your body, you are releasing literally a flood of neurochemicals in your brain that is the physical thing that happens, and I'm not talking about running a marathon, I'm talking about even taking a walk, a ten-minute walk, gets that flood of neurochemicals going.*

Is it different if you do get your heart rate up? Yes, it is. But the power starts with a ten-minute walk. The neurochemical flood starts with a ten-minute walk.

What is that flood of neurochemicals? It is dopamine, serotonin, adrenaline, endorphins, and growth factors. The first three, dopamine, serotonin, and adrenaline — those are what are going to make you feel great.

You've just given your brain this flood of neurochemicals that I like to call a neurochemical bubble bath for your brain. I love that image because if you move regularly, think of it as a regular bubble bath for your brain. These neurochemicals that are making you feel good, the growth factors go to your hippocampus, that is what's growing those brand-new hippocampal cells, and the power of exercise comes from that neurochemical bubble bath."

Rodney Terrell Kornegay is a Financial Advisor with New York Life and lives in Bridgewater, Massachusetts. Rodney experiences this firsthand and he says that while there are some days that are more productive than others, he finds that his "*most productive days start with a simple walk or run. I have noticed that the days that I complete some type of workout in the morning, the day ends more productively.*"

Science literally agrees with you, Rodney.

Trusting the science, I move my body first thing in the morning, and while I wait for class to start, I often make a pre-determined decision about how long I will stay in class that day.

What I *should* do is get started in class and work out with the goal of getting through the entire class. What I often do is decide in advance how long I will stay. Most of the OrangeTheory® classes I sign up for are an hour long, but on some days I only stay for thirty minutes. Other days, I stay for the full hour. This is often contingent on how much time I have, how tired I feel, and whether something at work is pulling me and making me stress about getting started.

Even thirty minutes at the gym is still better than nothing, and I will often focus on the workout that I need the most that day, whether it is strength training or cardio.

Another reason that I personally love working out in the morning is that, during the workout, I am staying hydrated and drinking a shit-ton of water. Yes, a shit-ton — a scientific term. Research shows that drinking water in the morning before eating or having coffee offers several scientifically supported benefits, rooted in hydration, digestion, metabolism, and even cognitive function. I'll cover more on that later when I'm ready to have my morning cup of coffee.

Before your first sip of coffee or bite of food, hydrate with a glass of water. This simple act replenishes lost fluids, kickstarts your metabolism, and primes your brain and digestive system for the day ahead. Science supports it, and your Perfectly Productive Day depends on it.

This idea aligns with what many health experts emphasize when they strip wellness back to its essentials. Dr. Rangan Chatterjee, a medical doctor and health expert who focuses on uncovering the root causes of chronic health issues, believes that meaningful improvements in health come down to four simple pillars: food, movement, sleep, and relaxation. None of them, he says, need to be complicated.

Take movement, as an example. Dr. Chatterjee has a five-minute strength workout that he does daily in his kitchen.

And you can too. It's an effective workout that everyone has time for.

Dr. Chatterjee wakes up early and heads into the kitchen. Unlike my quick and lazy Keurig coffee (we haven't made it that far together yet), Dr. Chatterjee is a self-proclaimed coffee aficionado. He grinds his coffee beans coarsely, preheats his French press, adds the grounds and hot water, and then he waits for it to steep.

At this point, Dr. Chatterjee sets a five-minute timer to ensure his coffee has steeped to perfection. And then Dr. Chatterjee does an effective five-minute strength training routine in his kitchen.

On his website named after him, Dr. Chatterjee states,

> *"Contrary to popular belief, you don't need to go to the gym to have an effective workout. My five-minute kitchen workout is an easy (and free!) way to incorporate strength training into your daily routine.*
>
> *Every day in my practice, my patients tell me they do not have time to exercise. Believe me, I understand this well. Modern life is busy! I, too, have a consuming job and young kids at home, so I know how precious spare time can be.*
>
> *My Five-Minute Kitchen Workout is something I actually started designing when I was a young kid. While my dinner was being warmed up, I would hit the deck and do press-ups and sit-ups until my food was ready!*

What I've discovered as an adult is that the kitchen can be a very productive place to exercise. Just think how often you find yourself in the kitchen throughout the day… waiting for something to boil or for the oven timer to go off. Instead of automatically reaching for your smartphone or the TV remote, why not use the time effectively?"

Dr. Chatterjee points out something critical about this five-minute workout routine. It is less about the effect it has on your body. Instead, it is about the effect that it has on your mind.

This five-minute morning workout is a keystone habit that helps you take on a productive mindset all day long. What this daily habit really does is answer the questions:

- *Do I trust myself?*
- *Can I rely on myself?*

Setting the goal to complete this daily routine and then succeeding in doing it affirms to yourself that you can do anything that you put your mind to. That you can trust yourself and you can rely on yourself.

Moving your body helps to move your mind.

What intention can you set, however small it may seem, and then succeed in proving to yourself that you trust yourself and you can rely on yourself? The 1% changes checklist, which can be found at www.perfectlyproductiveday.com/resources, will help you do just that.

Even if you do not work out at all, consider a micro step you could take to incorporate movement into the start of your day.

How is this all sounding to you? I hope it sounds doable. Now, let's get moving.

A Meditative Cleanse

Following the workout, I return home and take a shower. Often, at this time, most of my family is still asleep. As a result, I often shower in silence and use the time to meditate (in addition to the thirty minutes I meditated on the treadmill).

The definition of meditation is to ***pay attention***.

That's it.

We don't need fancy apps or teachers to help us meditate. We just have to be comfortable with paying attention.

Patricia De Fonte is a Trusts & Estate attorney, owner of De Fonte Law PC - Estate Planning With Heart®, serving clients throughout California. And I respect and admire her whole-heartedly. She leads a team of Trusts & Estate attorneys who handle their clients' needs *with heart,* and she is able to do that because she says that,

> *"My perfectly productive day starts with quiet time in the morning. A glass of water, a cup of coffee, go to the backyard without my phone, and just stare out into space. I like some quiet time before I let the world in."*

If that is not the definition of meditating, of **paying attention**, then I don't know what is.

Do you have a habit of meditating or just paying attention in the morning for a minute or two? If not, try it. This simple habit pays dividends immediately.

While in the shower after the gym, I often pay attention to how I am feeling and what I am feeling. I pay attention to what is on my mind. While the warm water is spraying down, and while I am breathing in the fresh air from the open window in our shower, I just let my thoughts flow. I pay attention to what smells I am smelling. I pay attention to the noises that I am hearing.

This quiet time is critical to my Perfectly Productive Day, and I am not alone. Jaime Lasater, an attorney in Round Rock, Texas, says,

> *"A quick morning walk, coffee, and some dedicated focus time to set intentions for the day and for the week and to create a strategy and schedule for projects and other work helps me kickstart my perfectly productive day."*

Dan Beck prioritizes twenty minutes every morning to pay attention to his breath. Isn't it super cool that your breath is both something that you can control and that can occur without any thought at all?

Mediation can be sitting on the floor of a quiet room, in a temple or monastery, in your shower, or while on a walk. Mine primarily occurs in the shower, which fits my available time for this daily practice and habit. It also leans into my creative side, which, you may recall from the introduction, is how this book came to be. Sitting with my own thoughts in the shower before ever consuming email, texts, the news, or social media.

Hold on a second. Before I lose you in thinking that this is what my morning looks like every day, don't you worry, I am also going to be explaining my Perfectly Unproductive Day, too. Because this is life and life happens, and a Perfectly Productive Morning does not happen 24/7/365. Hijacks to our day occur and we will also address those. I just wanted to make that clear before we continue with my shower meditation.

Once out of the shower, I throw on my cozy bathrobe and tie it around my waist. There are some mornings when nobody else in the house wakes up for still another thirty or forty minutes. There are other mornings when one or both of my children are already awake. Fortunately, on those mornings, they watch television quietly.

My favorite mornings are the ones where I walk out to the kitchen and the home is still very quiet.

Guarding and leveraging this precious morning time may be familiar to many of you. In fact, Dustie Robeson is the CEO and Founder of Springbook Partners, LLC, based in the San Francisco Bay Area. Dustie's company designs and produces comprehensive Estate Planning binders for its clients.

During the pandemic, Dustie developed a healthy morning routine that helped her through some unfamiliar days.

> *"I woke up before the rest of my family, and it felt like stealing a little piece of private time while all five of us were cocooned together. I would light a candle, do a ten-minute meditation, stretch, and do a quick free write. The meditation gave me a best practice to hold on to for the day. The free writing felt like it got my mind in gear. I woke up genuinely excited to get out of bed and made that time for myself. I can't help but think that it helped me transition into my days in the best ways possible — thoughtfully, grounded, and in touch with my creativity."*

Are you seeing a theme here?

For many, that quiet, peaceful time in the morning can set us up for a productive, impactful day. If it is not possible to wake up before everyone else in your home, then perhaps that peace comes to you at night when the house is still and quiet.

As we will repeatedly visit throughout this book, the Perfectly Productive Day does not necessarily start with the

Perfectly Productive Morning. It is cyclical and dependent on all of its parts.

On this Perfectly Productive Morning, I enter the kitchen, ready to make my delicious coffee. It seems crazy, but I have now been awake for almost two hours. I've journaled, exercised, been outside, and drank plenty of water. All of those healthy and scientifically proven productive habits before I've even looked at my phone or had any coffee.

Many experts, including Stanford neuroscientist Dr. Andrew Huberman, advise against drinking coffee immediately upon waking. Doing so can disrupt your body's natural cortisol rhythm — a hormone that helps you feel alert in the morning. Consuming caffeine too early can blunt this natural peak, leading to an energy crash later and even affecting sleep quality that night. Over time, this pattern may also affect mood stability and weight regulation by throwing off key hormones tied to stress and appetite.

Instead, delaying caffeine intake by 90 to 120 minutes after waking allows your body to wake up naturally and maintain more consistent energy throughout the day.

This is one of the reasons that I find my Perfectly Productive Day means getting up early and getting my workout done first. Because when I do not start with the workout and water intake, I almost always have coffee first thing in the morning.

Earlier, I also introduced Dr. Chatterjee and his kitchen workout while his French Press is steeping. While a cup of French Press coffee sounds wonderful at the surface level, I recognize that I am not a coffee snob. My Keurig makes good coffee quickly. That fits my life, and it is perfect for my busy morning. While the Keurig is warming up, I pour my creamer into the empty mug and place it on the Keurig platform to await the freshly brewed, scalding-hot cup of Joe.

Here's another little fun game or hack that I play to help support myself in what I know to be my Perfectly Productive Morning. I've already established that, just because I know it is the healthiest and most productive start to my day, I do not always get up and go to the gym. One of my favorite mugs to drink coffee out of happens to be a mug that I got from OrangeTheory® for Mother's Day one year ago. (Well, it used to be my favorite mug until I received my Perfectly Productive Day mug). I made a deal with myself. I am only allowed to use that mug if I have already gone to OrangeTheory® on that day. It's a simple strategy, and it is also an effective strategy.

In fact, while coaching one of my clients, Crissy, she mentioned that she wants to start ten minutes of strength training every morning. She was successful for the first few days, but — and you've been here before too — she lost the motivation. There wasn't a strong enough trigger or reward to support her new habit of performing ten minutes of weightlifting each morning.

I told her about my mug strategy. She lit up. She excitedly told me about a contribution she had made to an organization and that she had received a mug from it. She recognized that she was always a little sad when her husband did not make her coffee in that mug. We had the perfect reward to encourage her to get some exercise in the morning. And it worked. She even told her husband her strategy so he could help support the habit. If she wakes up and gets that exercise in, he will use that mug. If not, he will use a different mug. Isn't it funny how something as simple as a coffee mug can make a huge difference in our mood? Use that little hack to support your desired habits — this is an example of the 1% changes that you will be challenged with.

Once my morning cup of candy, uh, coffee, is ready, I walk over to the couch and set it down on the table next to my favorite seat on the couch. Most mornings, I crack open my book again before I do anything else. Typically, I like to read another chapter or two, or for about fifteen minutes. I call this my "Magical Moment" because I truly love reading in a quiet, cozy living room with my sweet coffee and no other distractions, noises, or people around.

On other mornings, this is the first time I look at my phone. Usually, it is just to check a few things before turning back to reading. Sometimes it gets sucked into some quick emails or social media.

On my Perfectly Productive Morning, I sit on the couch with my book and my coffee until about 6:30 a.m., and then, I grab my coffee, get up, and head back into my primary bathroom to get ready for the day.

Dress to Impress

Remember how I mentioned that I struggled with where to start this book? At what section makes the most sense? This is because here is another example where starting with the Perfectly Productive Evening Routine would make more sense. And I'll elaborate on this later in the book.

Waiting for me in the primary bathroom is my outfit for the day. Thank you last night Sarah, because I don't have to think about what to wear today – that decision has already been made for my Future Self.

After removing my robe and hanging it back on the hook, I spray my body again with body spray, put on the outfit for the day, and apply deodorant and perfume.

Next, I do something with my hair. Now, I will be honest. I've decided that, on most days, I want to spend about one to two minutes on my hair. This means I am either putting it up in a ponytail or half back with a clip.

For you, my amazing professional, doing your hair may be one of the most important things you do each day. How long does it take you? Are you sure? Have you actually timed yourself? Make sure, as you're building your Perfectly Productive Day, that you account for the actual time it takes to do your hair and don't underestimate it.

On the mornings when I have an in-person meeting or I am presenting to a group of awesome and esteemed professionals, like you, I often allow extra time to blow-dry and straighten my hair. Otherwise, this step in my morning routine is often pretty quick.

Finally, I put on my makeup, which takes me about five to ten minutes most mornings. There are some days that I am Pamela Anderson, circa 2025, and go au natural. It often depends on what is on the calendar that day. Also, I used to put my makeup on before doing my hair until someone taught me that it is better to put on the makeup after doing my hair so that you don't sweat it off when using those hot products on your beautiful mane. Fascinating…and so smart. See, I am also always open to learning things and being a student in life – that's the growth mindset.

Last, I put on my jewelry and take one final look at myself in the mirror. You look beautiful, Sarah. You're awesome, and you are going to have a great day!

CHAPTER 3

Navigating Real-Life Mornings

Before I dive into what my Perfectly Unproductive Morning looks like, I want to acknowledge what happens when we have children. I am sure that you remember those mornings. You are in a deep sleep, dreaming about that huge project at work, or that weird encounter at the grocery store, when your alarm goes off. Except your alarm isn't some pleasant melody on your phone. No, it is your infant screaming, your toddler screaming, or your elementary-school-aged child stomping around. (We know it isn't your teenager because they're still asleep right now.)

There is no such thing as a Perfectly Productive Morning, or designing a routine that does not involve reacting to the little human's needs. Being woken up by your kid's hooting and hollering is the new normal.

But it doesn't have to be.

Magan Dobson is a mother of three young daughters, a military wife, and a full-time working mom. She works as an Operations Manager for Novus Global.

Magan is also a superhuman and reads an average of 20 to 30 books per year. (I know this because she is a member of my unofficial book club, which you can learn more about on the Resources page on www.perfectlyproductiveday.com).

Recognizing that her Morning Routine is easily hijacked by her daughters' or her husband's needs, Magan says that *"waking up before my children to drink coffee and work for a few hours is key to starting my day productively."*

She says she also prioritizes tackling her most important tasks in the morning, when her energy is high, and schedules 'me' time throughout the week. She says,

> *"In addition to reading and walking, another thing I prioritize each week is taking adult jazz and adult tap classes at my kid's dance studio. It gives me a creative outlet and something that is just for me.*
>
> *I also find intentional downtime such as rewatching familiar shows like Grey's Anatomy and Scandal, which I use as a way to mentally recharge."*

Whether it is reading, walking, dancing, or watching reruns of your favorite show, prioritizing something for yourself is important. We are all familiar with the instructions that you should put on your own oxygen mask first, but how often are you practicing this act in real life?

Let's start now. What time does your precious child wake up? Take that time and roll the clock back even fifteen minutes. Set your alarm for that new wake-up time to enjoy this brief time to start your day off with your priorities and your best intentions. We already covered waking up and moving when the alarm goes off, so we no longer need to worry that you'll just snooze through that extra fifteen minutes. And, be prepared to also plan on going to bed at least fifteen minutes earlier. More on that when we discuss the Perfectly Productive Bedtime Routine together later.

Finally, be prepared to forgive yourself, because not every morning will go perfectly as planned. Let me set that example.

How One Scroll Stole My Morning

On one particular Thursday morning in September, my day started off right. I slept well and woke up at 4:30 a.m. to get ready for the gym. Aligned with my Perfectly Productive Morning, I got dressed and completed my ***Seven Perfectly Productive Day Primer*** questions. Then, as I put my toothbrush into my mouth to brush it, I shifted into my Perfectly Unproductive Morning. I checked Facebook on my phone.

Now, this is the moment that I wish I had a giant alarm that would go off, reminding me, warning me, that this is never going to help contribute to my Perfectly Productive Morning and my Perfectly Productive Day. (The same is true for checking email at this point.)

Scrolling through Facebook, I read a post from my best friend. The post had a sweet story and lovely pictures of her daughter celebrating her 8th birthday. It was posted six hours ago…yesterday. I missed my best friend's daughter's birthday.

And now, instead of enjoying my Perfectly Productive Morning and my workout, I am feeling guilty and mad at myself. And if you're thinking, well, at least you saw it. Right. But at 4:30 in the morning, I am not going to text my friend. I am already late to wish her daughter a Happy Birthday at this point; whether I decide to send it at 4:30 a.m. or 4:30 p.m., it is still a day late.

If I had waited until later in the morning to check Facebook, I would still have seen her daughter's birthday post, still have felt guilty, and still have been late wishing her a belated birthday greeting. The difference is that it would not have affected my Perfectly Productive Morning.

And that is describing a morning where I still did a lot of the actions that lead up to my Perfectly Productive Morning – getting outside, not drinking coffee before water, and moving my body – and yet, that one small unproductive and not advised action shifted my mood and my mindset. Imagine what happens when I completely screw up my Perfectly Productive Morning by not getting up at all when the alarm goes off. Well, let's imagine it together.

The Screw-the-Alarm Morning

Not every day goes as planned. This book, The Perfectly Productive Day, is to highlight the research and science that have proven what we need to do and *should* do to have a Perfectly Productive Day, and to try to develop a habit of doing it on most mornings. But, as we all know from personal experience, it is not always the reality. Sometimes, our day gets hijacked early, and we have a "Screw-the-Alarm" kind of morning.

And that happened to me on a particular Monday morning in October. When the alarm went off to go to the gym, I said, "Nope, not today!!!"

As I write this section on Monday morning, I have just woken up twenty minutes ago. This means I have not had any water, I did not go to the gym, I have not been outside, I did not write my **Seven Perfectly Productive Day Primer** questions in the journal, and I have already taken the first sip of my morning coffee. Yum.

And don't get me wrong, it is still early – it is 5:40 a.m. (I am a morning person), but this is not the morning that leads to a Perfectly Productive Day for me. This is my "contingency plan morning."

Let me break this down for you. I really have three types of mornings (during the week):

- My Perfectly Productive Morning is the one described in detail on that Tuesday, April 2nd, wherein I use **My Three Perfectly Productive Pushes** to act instead of thinking about acting.

   I wake up at 4:30 a.m., everything is lined up for me, and I am going to the gym. I write in the journal, get fresh air, drink water, and finish a workout. All of that occurs before I even have coffee.

   Upon arriving home (90 minutes after waking), I shower, then pour myself a cup of coffee and enjoy it while reading.

   After I've read for ten to twenty minutes, I might look at my phone.

- My *contingency plan for the morning* is to still wake up early – today was at 5:20 a.m. – but not do all of the things that I know benefit my Perfectly Productive Day like on that Monday morning we just discussed.

   On those days, I often skip journaling – why bother, I am already rebelling against the plan. I usually pour coffee and read shortly after waking up. Sometimes I check my phone, and sometimes I still stick to the plan and leave my phone in locked mode.

   These days, I am ruminating on my decision not go to the gym. I am trying to figure out an alternative time to be able to go, and most days that is unsuccessful, likely because I am already feeling fatigued from too many decisions or a plan. Usually, I am still reading while drinking my coffee or writing in the book like that particular Monday morning we just experienced.

- My Terrible, No Good, Very Bad, Totally Unproductive Morning is when I say, "screw it" and do the opposite of everything I know is best for me in the morning.

  I shut off my alarm – maybe even in the middle of the night when I decide that there is no way in Hell that I am getting up at 4:30 a.m. I keep drifting back to sleep until I absolutely have to wake up.

  When I do get up, I light fire to the journal – ok, I don't really, but I don't have the time nor the desire to write in it. I am usually rushing to get dressed, pour some coffee, and run out the door to my office. I feel foggy-headed – maybe from having a Perfectly Unproductive Evening if you know what I mean – or maybe from too much sleep (this can happen), or not prioritizing my morning goal of reading.

Being aware of these mornings helps me set my goal to have more Perfectly Productive Mornings each week than Terrible, No Good, Perfectly Unproductive Mornings. It is effective.

And, we've discussed it before, but since I often talk about my early mornings, I want to be clear about something. It isn't about the time that you wake up. There are many mornings when I still wake up early, but I don't invest in the habits that make up my Perfectly Productive Day. Your Perfectly Productive Morning is created and implemented based on the time that works for you to wake up – whether that is 4:30 a.m. or 9:30 a.m.

The Perfectly Productive Morning is simply doing the things that **you know you need** to do that ensure you have a Perfectly Productive Morning and a Perfectly Productive Day. So, I've explained what I need. What do you need?

Take a moment to think about this and answer it in the Perfectly Productive Day Workbook.

What do you need to live your Perfectly Productive Morning? What time do you need to wake up? What do you want to ensure you do (or do not do) each morning before the chaos of the day ensues? Identify it and start making the 1% changes to live that Perfectly Productive Morning whenever possible.

Reinforcement to Keep Going

I want to check in with you here. How are you doing? As you reflect on where you are right now, I want to remind you that you are not going to change overnight. That's why you and I are focusing on the 1% changes.

Whether you started reading The Perfectly Productive Day an hour ago or three months ago, you are succeeding. You are making progress towards being a more productive version of yourself.

As we discussed in the Limiting Beliefs section, your default thoughts were likely not positive. Maybe you were hard on yourself because it is taking too long to read to this point. Maybe you reflected on the Perfectly Productive Morning category and considered everything you have not tried or have not stuck to.

This book is about progress and not perfection. You are not behind. You are not failing. You are not a lost cause.

Napoleon Hill is the author of Think and Grow Rich, which was first published in 1960. Hill explains the story of

R. U. Darby and his uncle. During the gold-rush days, Darby and his uncle invested in machinery to drill and seek gold. After hitting some initial success, Darby and his uncle continued their quest. Ultimately, after some unsuccessful attempts, they decided to quit.

"One of the most common causes of failure is the habit of quitting when one is overtaken by temporary defeat."

Darby and his uncle sold all of their equipment to a junk man. That buyer was smart enough to seek expert counsel before giving up, and he benefited from it. With the help of a mining engineer, the junk man ended up finding millions of dollars' worth of gold, only three feet from where Darby and his uncle had given up.

They were so close, and they didn't even know it.

You, too, are so close. You are three feet away from your own success story, and you're reading this book for the expert advice. So don't give up now. *"Failure is a trickster with a keen sense of irony and cunning. It takes great delight in tripping one when success is almost within reach."*

Let's achieve that success together.

Design Your 1% Difference

One of the most powerful drivers of motivation and productivity is the feeling of making progress.

In their research on workplace performance, Harvard Business School professor Teresa Amabile and psychologist Steven Kramer coined the term *The Progress Principle* to describe how even small wins can lead to greater engagement, creativity, and overall job satisfaction. Their findings, published in *The Progress Principle: Using Small Wins to Ignite Joy, Engagement, and Creativity at Work*, highlight the importance of tracking progress and celebrating incremental achievements.

By focusing on forward movement—no matter how small—you can create a more productive and fulfilling workday.

Each of the six core categories of this book have 1% changes tied into that category, and you are able to access the 1% Changes Checklist at www.perfectlyproductiveday.com/resources or via the QR Code at the end of the book. These are the micro changes that you can make that, in whole, will help you create your Perfectly Productive Day. Sometimes the challenge is not even knowing which box to check to make progress. The idea is not to check the box for every 1% change, but to check the 1% changes that appeal to you.

Complete the accompanying workbook for the Morning Routine section. Review the 1% changes that you can make and pick one to three of them to make this week. You're making progress, you're making it easy and achievable, and you're doing great.

And now, it's time to get your butt out the door and on your way to the office, the store, or your work station at home. Let's talk about your Perfectly Productive Commute.

Commuting

. . . .

"You don't have to see the whole staircase, just take the first step."
- MARTIN LUTHER KING JR.

CHAPTER 4

Preparing for the Day Ahead

My first son was born in the summer of 2013, and I was fortunate enough to have an amazing four-month maternity leave. There was a part of me who would have loved to stay home and care for this adorable infant around the clock. At the same time, if I'm being truthful, I was excited to return to work, be around other adults, and go back to some normalcy.

Despite feeling that way, the first day back to work after maternity leave is often the hardest. There are so many mixed feelings and emotions about your choices, leaving your baby, and wondering if people will remember you at the office. The emotional roller coaster swirls around, and you feel all the feels: sad, guilty, scared, worried, nervous, anxious, and excited. There are so many unknown questions entering your mind, and it is impossible to organize them into one cohesive thought.

- *Did I make a gigantic mistake at work before I left, and it was uncovered while I was away?*

- *Is there enough milk for my son's caregiver?*
- *Did they decide to replace me at the office? Maybe they realized that I am no longer needed?*
- *Did I show his caregiver where the diapers and wipes are stored?*
- *Did they give my office away to someone else?*
- *My son has to have his binky at nap time. I hope his caregiver is nurturing enough to remember that. Maybe I should text her to remind her.*
- *Are they going to call me into Human Resources and let me go?*

On October 21, 2013, these thoughts and more were pedaling into my mind as I left to embark on my journey into the office on my first day back since giving birth.

Before maternity leave, my normal daily commute consisted of driving fifteen minutes to the Bay Area Rapid Transit (BART) station, taking a forty-minute BART ride into San Francisco, then a ten-minute walk to my office in the Financial District.

The morning of October 21, 2013, and the same morning that my maternity leave ended, was not a normal morning for Bay Area commuters. The news reported that BART employees were on a massive strike and that trains would not be operating. Many people would probably contact their employer and request an additional day (or two) off work to avoid the chaos that was going to occur throughout the freeways in the Bay Area.

But not me.

I was determined to get back to the office and face those unknowns – not to mention the fear that if I didn't go back on that first day, they would have a legal reason to let me go.

So, I found a carpool group that could take me to and from San Francisco. I remember everyone in that carpool being very shocked and supportive of my first day back at work after having a baby. I will always remember that commute at the butt crack of dawn on that cold October morning.

Of course, the reverse situation happened in March 2020 when COVID caused a nationwide shelter-in-place. You likely remember that shift when, like so many of us, we were faced with an entirely new commute. Or, more appropriately, a lack of commute.

That shift was challenging for many professionals, who now blended work and home life more intimately than before. The prior routine of getting dressed, leaving the house, and driving, walking, riding, or otherwise commuting to your office no longer existed. Now, your commute primarily consisted of rolling out of bed and making sure your top half looked presentable to your co-workers, without worrying about what you were wearing below your waist (business on top…uh, yoga pants on the bottom). Or it was figuring out which seat in your home was comfortable enough to sit in for eight-plus hours a day.

Years later, most of us have settled into a new routine and a new normal. There are, however, still some struggles with transitioning into and out of the workday, and that's what this section is about. We will cover two types of commutes that exist today: the actual commute (e.g., you're still traveling to your office on certain days) and the non-commute (e.g,. you're settling into your home office for the workday).

Cruise Control: Turning Your Car
Ride into a Productivity Win

For years, because of COVID, I did not leave my Shoffice (this is what I call my Shed-office). Then, in October 2022, a networking group I belong to began holding regular in-person meetings. I was back to the post-maternity leave commute of riding BART into San Francisco.

It's often too easy to jump into our car or step onto the train or bus without a plan of what exactly we will do during that commute. However, planning out the activities that would be most impactful during these times will help you be more productive, feel more accomplished, and get more done. A concept called temporal bundling or habit stacking.

Temporal bundling is the practice of combining present and future benefits into a single activity, allowing individuals to enjoy an immediate reward while also accomplishing a longer-term goal. The concept was introduced by behavioral scientists Katy Milkman, Julia Minson, and Kevin Volpp in a 2014 study.

For example, someone might only allow themselves to watch their favorite TV show (an immediate reward) while exercising at the gym (a long-term benefit), increasing the likelihood they'll follow through with the workout. Or, a commuter might choose to take public transportation while taking an online course they need to complete for professional credits.

In fact, my colleague and friend, Saja Raoof, recently did just that. Saja and I both belong to a networking group that meets at 7:00 a.m. At a recent meeting, I walked up to Saja and expressed how happy I was to see her, since she lives over an hour away. Saja responded with, "I almost didn't come."

She explained that she didn't sleep well the night before (she hadn't yet read about The Perfectly Productive Sleep in this book), and she has a rule not to drive long distances when she hasn't slept enough. When asked how she traveled this great distance (this is not a route where BART would be convenient at all), she said she hired an Uber.

"Brilliant," I said.

Audrey, another colleague and an amazing wealth advisor at Morgan Stanley, chimed in, "I take a self-driving car anytime I have to travel more than thirty minutes away." Audrey lives in San Francisco, and sometimes driving her car or losing her parking spot at home is not worth the trouble. (I know what some of you are thinking – "that's oh-so San Francisco of her.")

Audrey explained she loves the self-driving car because she often works while commuting to her destination, and this ensures she won't have an overly chatty driver on her commute. This way, she can use task batching – or temporal bundling – to accomplish the short-term goal of getting to her destination with the long-term goal of accomplishing things in her business.

While not always economically feasible, sometimes the investment in hiring a driver (or a driverless car) is a very smart and productive move.

Consider, for a minute, that you have something that you need to work on uninterrupted for an hour. Your calendar today is jammed packed with calls, meetings, and other commitments. The white space just does not exist on your calendar today.

Lucky you, you completed your Shut Down Routine during your Perfectly Productive Workday (more on that later), and you realized that you have to travel forty-five minutes each way to get to an important meeting or a client's destination. You were stressing about cramming it all in, and now you relax a little having decided to schedule a driver. You're so smart!

It is an expense but consider the value of your time. In his book "80/20 Sales and Marketing," Perry Marshall created the chart below showing the value of the tasks that you are doing.

$10 per hour tasks	$100 per hour tasks	$1,000 per hour tasks	$10,000 per hour tasks
Running errands	Solving a problem for a prospective or existing customer	Planning and prioritizing your day	Improving your unique selling proposition
Talking to unqualified prospects	Talking to a qualified prospect	Negotiating with a qualified prospect	Creating new and better offers
Cold-calling	Writing an email to prospects or customers	Building your sales funnel	Repositioning your message and position
Building and fixing stuff on your website	Creating marketing tests and experiments	Judging marketing tests and experiments	Executing "bolt from the blue" brilliant ideas
Doing expense reports	Managing pay-per-click campaigns	Creating pay-per-click campaigns	Negotiating major deals
Working "social media" the way most people do	Doing social media well (this is rare)	Doing social media with extreme competence (this is very rare)	Selling to high-value customers and groups
Cleaning, sorting	Outsourcing simple tasks	Delegating complex tasks	Selecting team members
Attending meetings	Customer follow up	Writing sales copy	Public speaking
Source: "80/20 Sales and Marketing," by Perry Marshall			© HBR.org

The $10 per hour column should also include driving in certain situations where your time is spread thin. I'm not talking about the daily short trips that are necessary; instead, we are talking about the longer commutes where you might consider that your time is more valuable than your money.

More recently, I've been hiring drivers for longer commutes to work-related events, and it has paid dividends in return. I understand, for reasons we do not need to get into, that hiring a driver for commutes may not be practical. As such, we should also explore the situations where you have to drive yourself and, of course, you need to operate the vehicle safely.

Steering Toward Productivity

What would this Perfectly Productive Commute section be without also discussing the more realistic commute – driving yourself – since not everyone is in a situation where you can hire someone to chauffeur you around?

For those of you who drive frequently, maybe even daily, I recommend considering task batching on some of your drives and finding something productive to do during the drive. This is not intended to be a formula or a rigid routine. Instead, it is meant to give you ideas for what you could do during some of your daily commutes to build habits and get things done without feeling as though you need to find more time. You do not have to do it every day, but even doing something two or three days per week during your commute could benefit you in the long term.

Remember when I mentioned in our conversation about the Perfectly Productive Morning that I read every day? If reading is of interest to you, then your commute is an excellent time to knock out some audiobooks. Even a fifteen-minute commute in each direction means you could still finish an audiobook roughly every two weeks.

Sami Azhari is a criminal defense attorney in Chicago. Sami is an avid reader and likes to make the most of his time to get caught up on his reading. Brilliantly, Sami reads both physical books, and he also downloads the audio version as well. Why? Because if he is reading, say in the morning, and he is about to jump into the car, he switches to the audio version so he can continue the story, even while commuting in the car. I love this task batching technique and habit!

Katie Burke is a family law attorney and workplace investigator in San Francisco. In 2024, Katie joined my annual 24 Books in 2024 Book Club. After she added the goal of reading more to her plate, Katie admitted that she was struggling between listening to audiobooks (her new habit) and listening to her favorite podcasts (her other interest) while on her commute. What to do?

I recommended she design a clear habit based on the direction she was going on her commute. In other words, heading into the office on the bus in the morning, she listens to her audiobook. Then, on her route home, she listens to a podcast. She is able to invest time in both activities she enjoys, make progress toward her goals, and use her commute time effectively and wisely. She also doesn't get stuck in the decision-fatigue cycle we often experience, which hijacks our plans and causes us to freeze (and then doomscroll).

She loved this idea. And the best part is that within about two to three weeks, it becomes a habit. She just presses play in the appropriate app on her phone to listen to the book on her way into the office, and she starts the latest episode of her favorite podcast on the way home.

I am guessing that you, too, are hoping to find ways to be more productive, and I am also assuming that you enjoy reading or listening to audiobooks since you are reading this book. But maybe you're more interested in podcasts or educational seminars that you can listen to while commuting. Even sometimes using this time to go into deep thought in a silent car can be a productive and healthy use of this time.

I even knew someone who would use their commute time to have a conversation with AI. He would initiate a chat with AI and ask it to converse with him while commuting the hour into his lab.

Whatever resonates with you, consider batching the task of driving or commuting with something that you need or want to get done and that can be done while safely operating a vehicle.

In the Perfectly Productive Workday section, we will dive deeper into multitasking and why that is ineffective. You cannot do two cognitively demanding tasks at the same time. Driving while reading a paperback book is not advised. Neither is driving and texting nor looking at email. However, driving and listening to something is often safe. Just be sure to hit play before you put your car into gear, and just be prepared to hit pause if you need a moment to think.

You've probably seen the memes or comics about having to turn your music down to find a parking spot. It's true, right? Sometimes, we need to focus when we are circling a parking lot or if someone cuts us off unexpectedly.

That is because you are now asking your brain to perform a cognitively demanding task. Naturally, your brain cannot process the music playing or audiobook talking while focused on figuring out the best parking spot, or if something unexpected and alarming happens on the road.

You have likely been driving for a long time, and it is so familiar that it is a habit. The repetitive and familiar activities of accelerating, changing lanes, following traffic lights, and cruising around do not activate your reticular activating system. All of these actions behind the wheel are habits by now. But, as soon as something out of the ordinary occurs, anything new or unfamiliar, then your brain becomes hyper-focused. And that means it cannot process all of the inputs – the audio playing with what is going on on the road.

So, if you drive to work or if you are otherwise in the car frequently, maybe consider what the Perfectly Productive Commute means for you. Maybe it is just listening to your favorite upbeat jams or comforting classical music. But if your goal is to get more reading done, or to catch up on your favorite crime podcast, or listen to an educational webinar (think CLE, CPE, or CMEs), then consider that some of your daily commute time is the perfect opportunity to accomplish a lot without it feeling as though you are losing time.

CHAPTER 5

Commuting with Purpose

I f your commute includes riding on a bus, subway, or train, or otherwise taking a form of transportation that does not require your cognitive mind, then consider how to be productive during that commute. Obviously, unlike driving, you may be able to do something with your hands, on your computer, or on your phone.

Thinking back to the time when my sons were infants, my BART ride would often consist of catching a forty-minute shut-eye or catnap (or as the men in my life call it, "just closing my eyes for a few minutes"). There were times when I'd wake myself up snoring. This was just a season in life when I wasn't getting a full night of sleep, nor was I getting consistent sleep, and my commute was a productive time to catch an extra sleep cycle. If you're in that season of your life right now, then go for it! Sleep is critical, and it may be the best use of your commute time to just relax and rest before you need to perform all day.

These days, I am fortunate enough to be able to follow the Perfectly Productive Sleep (most nights,) which means I am fully rested if and when I am commuting anywhere. As such, when I commute, I often choose to work on something that I might be procrastinating on and/or something that I can make an impact on. By selecting only one thing to do, it helps me focus on it because I'm in a different environment, and I feel as though I am maximizing that time. For example, I will often write the Firm Focus Productivity Hacks while on the train. It takes about thirty to forty minutes to write and edit it. The perfect time to crank it out without feeling as though it was prioritized over client work.

Bev Moranetz, CPO®, owns Streamline Organizing in Denver, Colorado. Bev admits she has a habit that is not necessarily a healthy habit in the morning, she processes email twice a day — in the morning before her day gets rolling, and in the evening before her personal time starts.

Recognizing that doing so in the morning is not best practice, Bev says,

"I know, you're not supposed to process email in the morning, but I like to read my newsfeeds, respond to any critical emails, and take care of quick tasks (David Allen's two-minute rule) before the day gets started, and that helps me feel settled."

What I hope you're taking away from our time together in this book is that we are merging best practices for a Perfectly Productive Day with realistic habits and recommendations by others. If I were coaching Bev, I would recommend that she postpone checking the emails until she was on her Perfectly Productive Commute. She would still feel settled, clearing her emails before she "gets to work," but she would also protect her Perfectly Productive Morning by waiting until she has been awake for at least thirty to sixty minutes before exposing her brain to external noise, information, and demands.

Revisiting your commute on a train, subway, or other transportation, at this time, you might be thinking, "well sometimes I don't have a reliable internet connection on the bus, or sometimes I don't get a seat."

Those are all excuses. If you have goals or a Trusted System (more on that in the Perfectly Productive Workday but for now it basically means a reliable To-Do list), you can always cherry-pick something to make progress on that doesn't require internet access and that you could do without a seat on the train.

Maybe you are interested in reading more. Plan ahead and pack your book.

Perhaps there is a podcast or class you can listen to. Bring earbuds and tee it up as the train takes off.

You could finish a continuing education class or training required for your profession on route to your destination.

You could save a document to your desktop and work from that copy until you have internet access again.

If you have contacts in your network you have been meaning to follow up with, draft the emails, save them in your drafts folder, and send them when you're back online. A little planning ahead will help you maximize that time.

If any of these suggestions sparked interest, that's great. Don't beat yourself up if you've never thought of them before. We often get stuck in a routine. Psychologists call this **habituation**, the tendency for repeated, non-threatening experiences to gradually stop capturing our attention. That's why we sometimes need to shake things up or have someone step in and recommend an alternative activity.

If none of these suggestions speak to you, then consider just meditating on your next commute. Remember, meditating means to pay attention. Look up and pay attention to what is going on around you. Studies have proven that you will feel more productive and happier if you observe others, smile, and sit in silence rather than scrolling your phone or reading the news. Practice being a little curious. What are others doing? What are they wearing? Do you notice any styles, colors, or patterns that you like? Do you see the same people on a regular basis? Have you smiled first?

The commuter who pays attention, smiles, observes, and practices being present will walk into work ready to tackle the day.

The commuter who scrolls their phone and soaks up social media, the news, and other depressing or unrealistic snapshots of someone else's life will feel tired, drained of energy, and will perform less productively when they get to their desk.

When you think about the Future You, which commuter will you be?

Great, your first step starts today.

During any commute – driving, taking the train, walking – many people have their heads down and their eyes buried in their phones. We have all done it. I've done it at times, and I try to catch myself in the moment. It really does not feel good.

We are addicted to our phones and often return to them the second we get bored to see what else is interesting. We crave that dopamine hit. But there are so many other options regarding what to do that are significantly more productive and will make you happier.

Even doing nothing on your commute is better than mindlessly scrolling social media on your phone. You could stare into space and dream a little. You could shut your eyes and relax. You could use this time to meditate. All of these options will help your mindset, your productivity, and your happiness for the rest of the day.

A study conducted by Nicholas Epley of the University of Chicago Booth School of Business and Juliana Schroeder of the Haas School of Business at the University of California Berkeley examined the relationship between social interactions and happiness during daily commutes. Participants were divided into two groups: one was instructed to commute as usual, while the other was encouraged to strike up a conversation with a fellow passenger on the train. Those who engaged in conversation consistently reported a more positive experience and greater happiness than those who kept to themselves.

Although many commuters initially assumed talking to strangers would be awkward or unwelcome, the findings showed otherwise. Brief social interactions enhanced participants' overall satisfaction with their commute and emotional well-being. The study highlights the unexpected benefits of small, intentional acts of connection in everyday settings, suggesting that even fleeting conversations with strangers can contribute meaningfully to happiness.

As you commute, consider if there is something that interests you and give it a try. Even talking to strangers has been shown to boost your mood and make you more productive. Put it to the test. I challenge you to give it a try tomorrow and talk to that middle-aged man who always wears the fedora or the woman with the cute purse. You might just meet someone who could change your life.

The Power of a Purposeful Transition

For many of us, March 2020 marked a period in time that so much in our lives changed when COVID was widespread, and the shelter-in-place was instated. For some, it was drastic changes and incredibly unfortunate results. For others, not much changed.

Commuting to work, and often five or more days per week, was suddenly stripped of most professionals. Now, they were not commuting at all, or only 40 percent of the time, compared to before March 2020.

For many professionals, their entire working life prior to March 2020 consisted of a commute that was an unspoken, yet familiar, transition from home life to work life. And while we can never draw a box around each of these lives and create separation (it is work/life balance, not work/life separation), the commute prior to March 2020 helped your mind move from the challenges and stresses of the home walls and ease you into the expectations of work life. And vice versa on the reverse commute.

Suddenly, those walls collided and work/life imbalance was created. Professionals, like you and me, were at work when they were at home. You could work in your kitchen, living room, bedroom, or on your front porch. In fact, you had to. You had to sometimes find a new place to work throughout the day to separate your need to focus from your partner's loud virtual call. You had to work from under a table to hide from your children, who were now home-schooled.

Work hours became any time of the day that you could "clock in" and get a few things done before you were inter-rupted again.

Some of you have settled into a new, comfortable, and familiar routine. Similarly, some of you who are still living this work/life imbalance and really suffering from it. A twenty-four-hour period just means there are twenty-four hours to try and fit it all in. A little work here, get the shopping done there, drive the kids to practice here, working off of your steering wheel or in the dance studio lobby. Prep, eat, and clean up after dinner. Answer some more emails. Relax on the couch. Log in to get that memo drafted. Crash for the night.

You see, this non-commute feeds into a scenario consisting of everything you need to get done at work, comingled with personal responsibilities. It's tiring and it often translates into a poor night of sleep. That poor night of sleep makes your morning routine suffer. Which results in a vicious cycle of designing your Perfectly Unproductive Day. As I said before, I struggled with where to start this book, because I truly look at this book, this 24-hour period, this day in your life, as a circular event. And maybe your Perfectly Productive Day starts here. With changing your non-commute.

We have already covered how your commute could be an intentional time and routine. Suppose you start work at 8:30 a.m. Hold yourself true to that start time for work, even if you work from home and don't need to actually commute anywhere. Keep your computer in a specific spot within your home and dedicate that space to working. Even if you need to move around while working, I'd still recommend having only a few designated work areas. Perhaps it is your desk set-up and the counter where you're able to stand. It should not be those places, the couch, your bed, and on the floor of your kid's bedroom. Find two spots (maybe three if you like a spot outside as well), and those are your designated work zones. It creates healthy boundaries, which helps your brain understand when and where you should be working versus where you should be spending quality time with your family.

Let me challenge you here for a moment. When you worked at the office, did you move around a lot? Did you go up to your assistants' workspace and take over because you needed a change of scene? Likely not. You probably had your office or workspace, a conference room you'd use at times, and one other common space you'd sit in periodically. Limit it to the same three choices at home, too.

When it is time to go to work, create a habit that indicates to your brain that you are transitioning into and out of work. Maybe, just before you start work at 8:30, you take a ten-minute walk. As we discussed earlier, numerous studies have shown that even a ten-minute walk can boost your productivity. Maybe you turn on a specific light on your desk to indicate you are now working.

Maybe you read for fifteen minutes, and that is your fake commute, telling your brain that you are now shifting from the Perfectly Productive Morning Routine into starting work at that designated spot in your home. Maybe it's waiting to have your coffee until it is time to start work. You take that first sip when you're at your computer and ready to punch the clock. Although be careful here. As you learned in my contingency plan morning, when I do not go to the gym, I like my coffee first thing in the morning, so I would easily create a habit of coffee first thing and working first thing when I wake up. Not the best habit for me.

I know this seems silly, but while our brains have evolved and will continue to grow and change thanks to neuroplasticity, they are still a childlike version of us. Our brains are happiest when we create boundaries, habits, and expectations that can be stored in our reticular activating system and happen automatically. Our brains are happiest when they don't have to think too hard.

If you start the habit of taking a ten-minute walk each day before starting work, you will, in a month or less, find yourself naturally transitioning into and out of the workday through that joyous activity.

If you read before you start work, you could learn so much, and you'd feel productive first thing in the morning.

If you sat down to enjoy your healthy breakfast at the dining room table and practiced being present, you would carry that positivity and a clear mind into your top project for the day.

Today, my commute is a non-commute. My Shoffice is located in my backyard, and each night I lock the Shoffice door and hang the key on a hook near our back door. During my evening non-commute, it indicates to me that I am done working for the night.

Then, in the morning, sometimes with my coffee in hand, I walk through my garden and unlock my Shoffice door. I turn on my computer to start my workday. Waiting for me at my desk is a perfect roadmap of what needs to be prioritized that day. This helps me ensure that I am getting that top priority project done first thing, and we will cover more on that in the Perfectly Productive Workday. See you there.

The Day That Starts You

Not every commute will be productive or enjoyable.

On this cold December morning, I am commuting to San Francisco. My Workday was hijacked in the afternoon yesterday, and I did not prepare enough for my meeting this morning. My contingency plan is to prepare for the meeting on the train into the city.

Based on what I know to be true, it should be easy to grab a seat on the train, and the hotspot on my phone should work just fine. Boy, was I wrong.

Arriving at the station, I noticed the overly crowded platform. Great. It turns out the prior train was taken out of service, so this train will be more crowded than usual. I am trying not to panic, as it is essential that I sit down to prepare for this meeting on my laptop.

No such luck.

I walk onto the already full train with the other riders at my station's platform. Not only is there no seat available, but there is barely enough room to breathe. This has turned into the Perfectly Unproductive Commute.

While attempting to prepare on my phone (which is never easy or productive for me), I realize that cell service is quite spotty today because of the weather. What should have taken me about fifteen minutes on the laptop has now taken the entire forty-five-minute train ride to complete, and also put me in a funk.

All I can think about now is how I set myself up for this by not prioritizing the prep yesterday afternoon, and now I am living a reactive and stressful moment, and I've put myself in a time debt. This is another reminder that all parts of the day support your Perfectly Productive Day.

And those moments are not exclusive to a true commute and can even happen in a virtual world commute situation. Let's hypothesize.

Everything seems to be going wrong today. After having had a terrible night of sleep, you roll over in bed and grab your phone. Immediately, you see a gazillion messages from your boss that you need to address. Your partner is awake and helping with the kids.

While still lying in bed, you answer a few emails from your boss. Sluggishly, you sit up and throw the covers off your body. You throw your feet on the floor and sit there for a minute. So many thoughts run through your head, but most aren't healthy or productive. The thoughts are swirling, trying to figure out what the most important thing is to do today. After all, what you think about doesn't matter anymore because you feel as though you have no choice but to immediately get to work responding to your client's or your boss's asks.

You move into the common area of the home and say hello and good morning to your family while grabbing whatever coffee mug is clean and available. You sit down at the table, pop open your computer, and immediately start responding to emails. That continues until you realize an hour later that you haven't even brushed your teeth or had a moment to think about anything that you, your body, or your mind might need today.

Your partner got the kids out the door and to school. But you now see that they forgot their lunch or the permission slip for the field trip due today. So you're going to need to take it over to them this morning. Sigh.

There is no commute. There is no transition from sleep or home life into work life. There is just jump right in without knowing the temperature of the water.

And it sucks. It totally sucks.

It feels like you are a slave to your work. Ironically, these are also the days that often end up running late into the night or the days in which you feel as though you cannot catch up.

For this reason, creating a transition or a "commute" – whether you truly have one or not – is essential to ensuring you have a Perfectly Productive Day.

Checking Your Pulse on Your Commute

Now, before we go into where we commuted to, WORK, let's briefly talk about the commute from work back to home. As we talked about earlier, many people miss out on the opportunity that the commute really is because their commutes are like movie previews, easily ignored and not intentional. However, when your goal is to have a Perfectly Productive Day, you cannot just decide to no-show or unintentionally navigate it.

I love the way Benjamin Franklin puts it, "Lost time is never found again." That is how you and I should both look at our commutes. Those who have perfectly productive days take that quote to heart and see that time as a treasure trove of opportunities to do their work and homework well.

When it comes to the commute from work, it's important to check your pulse. I don't mean this literally, so you can move your two fingers away from your wrist or neck. What I mean is to take a pause and use the time wisely. Ask yourself questions. Take inventory. For example, what did you decide to do during your commute? Were you like Katie and set an intention for what you would do? Are you present like we talked about in the morning routine, where you can say how your commute is going? Did you find an activity you enjoy while driving home? Are you finding productive projects to work on while on the train? Did you build in a clear transition from workday to home life after shutting your office door and walking down the hall to your living room?

Bev Moranetz says that she looks at her task list and highlights the things that she knows she can accomplish that day, both business & personal. For example, she can hit an errand on the way to a client.

Maybe, like Bev, you were able to hit up a few errands on the route home. Whatever it is, this is a good time to reflect on what has changed in your commute, if anything, and if it is working for you. Everyone's commute is a little different, and how you choose to maximize that time is unique to you. That could mean getting productive work done, catching up on a podcast or show, taking a course, or just sitting quietly and reflecting on your day.

Whatever you choose to do, have a pleasant commute home because the evening routine is waiting on the other side of that workday. Speaking of workday, that is where we're headed next.

Workday

. . . .

*"The key is not to prioritize
what's on your schedule, but
to schedule your priorities."*

- STEPHEN R. COVEY

CHAPTER 6

Finding Purpose in Your Work

Ever since I was a young girl, I was excited to enter the workforce and was likely always destined to be an entrepreneur. It was second grade when I knew I wanted to become either a teacher or an attorney. Yes, I recognize the irony that one would pay next to nothing and the other had the potential to pay well.

During most of my childhood, I was always playing school in my room and creating business opportunities. Some days I would be teaching my friends, my sister, my Barbies, or my stuffed animals. Other days, I found small but meaningful ways to build a business, from a lemonade-and-popcorn stand at the end of my country road driveway to a babysitting business that began with persistence and lasted until I left for college.

My company now, Firm Focus, is the result of merging everything I am, everything I've learned, and everything I've experienced into those two words: **Firm** and **Focus**. It touched on my long-time desire to be a teacher and forever interest in working in law. It leveraged my entrepreneurial spirit from an early age.

I am fortunate enough today to go to work each morning and put into practice the same skills, habits, and behaviors that I encourage in my clients. And it's the sum of all of this that also led to the creation of this book and the words on this page.

The work we do is aimed at helping busy, smart professionals like you find passion in their work. It is about creating some boundaries or expectations for themselves at work to ensure they focus on the right things, and then can separate themselves from work when they want to be present at home or with their social life. It is about using tools and systems to keep them productive and on track.

I am guessing you're reading this because you, too, have a lot of amazing skills, interests, and experience to bring to your career, but you often feel like you didn't accomplish anything on a particular day. Or you feel as though you are on the verge of burnout. You want to find ways to live your Perfectly Productive Day, and that relies heavily on how you live your Perfectly Productive Workday.

Let's explore how structure, intention, and self-awareness can transform the chaos of your current busy professional life into a focused, fulfilling, and high-impact routine.

The small decisions we make daily add up to either clarity or overwhelm. Which will you choose? Who do you want to be? Let's dive into your Perfectly Productive Workday together.

From Gavel to Guitar: The Power of Pursuing Passion

In 2024, I enrolled in an incredible business development coaching program led by my friend, colleague, and business coach,

Rudhir Krishtel. Also attending that program was a growing partner at a law firm who practiced in employment defense. His name was Craig. Stay with me, it gets more interesting.

Investing time, money, and a lot of mental headspace into that program helped me grow my company. In 2024, Firm Focus's first employee was hired. In that same year, we grew by bringing on two additional coaches (besides me) to the Firm Focus team.

The power of the program challenged me to consider what I really wanted and how to get there.

Now, Craig was experiencing the same training and coaching as I was, but of course exploring his own life and dreams and what he wanted his growth to look like. During the program, Craig bought a mobile bar. He bought a mobile bar and planned to start attending events and festivals to sell his signature cocktails.

During our Zoom meetings, Craig would often have his camera on and be engaged in the session. Hanging behind him on his wall were a plethora of guitars. Craig, you see, loved music. And while he is clearly an intelligent, high-functioning, and interesting attorney, he is also creative and enjoys being a musician and around music.

And so, six months after starting the Krishtel Circles business development program, Craig, who is still practicing law, found joy and love in transitioning his career to focus on the music industry. And now that Craig is passionate about what he does every day, we can help him design a Perfectly Productive Workday.

Loving What You Do for Work

You see, a Perfectly Productive Workday will never develop if you aren't doing something you enjoy. If you hate your career and dread your workday every day, then you won't invest time and energy into some of the strategies that are discussed in this book, *The Perfectly Productive Day.*

And if you don't invest in these strategies and find joy in your workday, then you won't sleep well. And you won't get up and drink water before coffee. And you will likely never invest in the small steps needed to start creating your Perfectly Productive Day.

So, let's start this section with one critical question:

Do you love what you do?

For a moment, set aside external factors in your answer, such as parental influence, student loan debt, financial needs, or other pressures.

Do you truly love what you do?

If your answer is an undeniable YES and you love what you are doing, then awesome! Let's keep going to help you create the Perfectly Productive Workday.

If not, let's explore that for a bit. I encourage you to pause for a minute here.

Like Craig, I have worked with clients who discovered that their time-management challenges at work stemmed from no longer loving what they were doing.

In some situations, like Craig, they were in the wrong industry altogether. For other clients, they were at the wrong company or working in the wrong practice group at a law firm.

Others, despite being happy with their profession, were doing more and more of the type of work that they didn't like, such as more research when they enjoy the writing. Or more desk work, when they loved being out there and networking.

If this is resonating with you, and you are feeling as though you need to explore what would truly make you happy in your profession, then I recommend you visit the Perfectly Productive Day Workbook now.

The Perfectly Productive Workbook includes a worksheet in the Workday section to help you explore what you should really be doing. This isn't just a reading book; this is a ***Take Productive Action Book***. So, pretend I inserted that worksheet into the pages right here. Put a bookmark flag at the top of this page to come back here once you complete the Perfectly Productive Workbook to find out if, instead of being an Employment Defense Litigator, you are really meant to find your inner Taylor Swift.

If you don't enjoy what you do, the best strategies will fall flat. Finding purpose in your work is a necessary precondition to building a truly productive day. When you're ready, come back to learn how you can create your Perfectly Productive Workday.

CHAPTER 7

Structuring a Productive Workday

Are you ready to start that Perfectly Productive Workday? You've had a Perfectly Productive Morning (or maybe not this morning, but that's ok, you can always reset). You've enjoyed your Perfectly Productive Commute and listened to your favorite podcast, worked on that sticky project, or enjoyed the quiet in your car and used that time to meditate – to pay attention and be present.

Now you are walking into your office or settling into your comfy chair at your desk. What do you see? Has the Yesterday-You set the Today-You up for success? Or are you immediately feeling overwhelmed, stressed, and behind? Are you immediately beating yourself up because there is so much that you need to get done?

That's going to change today (or whatever day that you and I finish talking about your Perfectly Productive Workday). Because we care about the Tomorrow-You now, and we want her to walk into her office or sit at her desk and feel empowered and motivated. We want her to feel in control. We want her to feel eager and ready to get started on her Perfectly Productive Workday. So, let's discuss what that looks like.

We are back to that Perfectly Productive Day on Tuesday, April 2nd. I've just finished my Perfectly Productive Morning Routine (meditate, gym, coffee, and reading) and I've enjoyed my Perfectly Productive Commute (unlocking my back door and walking through my garden and into my Shoffice)

After unlocking and opening the door to my Shoffice, I am greeted by the gift that Yesterday-Me left.

My desk is clear of any messy paperwork or files. My favorite pen and highlighter lay next to my computer mouse, ready to support me with my Perfectly Productive Workday. My computer has been shut down the night before and is asleep. Shutting the computer down at night achieves two critical goals:

1. The computer itself has the opportunity to rejuvenate and work more effectively the next day.
2. Closing out of all tabs, apps, and documents ensures I've closed my mind of those things at the end of the previous day.

Today is a new day, and I can design it in a way that supports the Perfectly Productive me, despite how yesterday turned out. I'm ready to reset and be the best version of me today. Let's talk about how you can design your day the way you want it to turn out, before your day designs you.

Next to my computer, I have a rolling cart with a tabletop that sits at arm's length. On top of that table is a notepad containing the architectural design for my workday. Thank you, Yesterday Me, because Today Me does not have to decide or waste my cognitive thinking on what to do. Since Yesterday Me helped me plan and prioritize my day, I get to invest my morning energy into *doing* it instead of *thinking* about doing it.

Researchers estimate that adults make up to 35,000 decisions each day, ranging from small, unconscious choices to larger, deliberate ones. While the exact number is debated, studies from Cornell and work by experts like psychologists Daniel Kahneman and Roy Baumeister support the idea that our brains are constantly making decisions, contributing to mental fatigue and the need for intentional routines.

This is why you and I are discussing "intentional" routines and designing your workday in a way that helps you create decisions within the details of the work instead of on what you should be working on. Otherwise, when you arrive to start your workday, instead of jumping right in, you still need to make a decision about what to focus on. This initial tough decision often leads to paralysis, and that paralysis results in you doing the easy (and not important) task because your brain is begging you for a break – and your day hasn't even begun.

You aren't going to do that anymore, *right?*

Right. So, you and I are in my Shoffice on Tuesday morning, April 2nd, and it is currently 7:00 a.m. My first meeting is at 8:30 a.m. That means I have ninety minutes of open time on my calendar. This is intentional and a result of the routines and boundaries created to guard that space on my calendar.

Jeff Windsor is an attorney and mediator in Silicon Valley, California, and Hawaii. In response to ensuring he has a Perfectly Productive Workday, Jeff says,

> *"I monitor my energy levels. For example, mornings are my most productive times. As such, I don't schedule any networking meetings in the morning. Those are saved for the afternoons when my energy is lower. The morning is best for me to write."*

Many mornings, I also guard that time because that is when I am most productive. Since you and I are being honest with each other, I want to share that there are mornings when I do not use that time productively – and usually I end up beating myself up or regretting the decision I made at the start of my day. We will discuss that further when we look at my Perfectly Unproductive Workday. Most days, however, I recognize the importance of utilizing that time to work on that most important project. By doing so, it ensures that anything I get done for the rest of the day feels like icing on the cake… and this girl loves icing (yes, even fondant icing).

You and I will later go into details about the habits that prevent us from getting that most important project done during this Deep Work time – behaviors such as procrastination, paralysis, and welcoming the distractions.

For now, the first step is to ensure there is time on the calendar and that you have designed the space to get focused work done early in your day. Let's dive into the three-step process to The Perfectly Productive Workday.

3 Step Process to the Perfectly Productive Workday

You've got the structure. Now it's time for the steps. Before we jump in, though, let's emphasize one important thing: the Perfectly Productive Workday is not about perfection. It's about putting the right things in place so what truly needs to get done has the best chance of happening. Productivity is often less about motivation and more about having supportive structures and intentional steps. The three steps we'll cover in this chapter offer a simple way to navigate the part of the day that often brings the most stress. Let's dive in.

Step 1. Dear Future Me: You're Welcome

What does a typical day look like on your calendar? Is it wide open – you do not have many meetings, phone calls, or appointments? Or is it jammed up with back-to-back engagements and commitments?

In either scenario, the Future You would highly benefit from holding Deep Work blocks of time on your calendar. If you're thinking, "But, I don't know what I will need that for." That's ok, and that's normal. You do not need to know today what the Future You will use that time for. What is important is that we anticipate that she will benefit from having that space held to use that time on something that becomes critical and important on that day, instead of allowing something insignificant to hijack the workday.

Let's connect this to the present moment. Assuming today is a workday, have you looked at the calendar to see what is on it?

For some of you, it might be empty. Usually, those are the people who do not have a lot of meetings, but still have a lot of important work to get done, nonetheless. We will come back to you a little later when we talk about the habits tied to getting the work done (procrastination, paralysis, distractions, etc.)

For those of you who take a peek at your calendar and see multiple meetings, appointments, and commitments on it. Your calendar looks like a game of Tetris — every block perfectly aligned, no gaps, no air. Just one immovable piece dropping after another, faster than you can catch your breath.

I get it. Sometimes my calendar looks like that.

But what if you could turn your calendar from a relentless game of Tetris into something more like Jenga — where intentional gaps between the blocks create balance, flexibility, and room to breathe? And ideally, before it all comes crashing down.

You can.

Right now.

You know what your typical day and week look like, so you will need to modify this recommendation to fit your commitments, needs, and demands. My recommendation is to place a few recurring blocks on your calendar to get Deep Work done. Let me break it down for you and me.

- Open your digital work calendar on Outlook or Gmail (or whatever calendar application you rely upon).
- Consider which days of the week are best for Deep Work time. My suggestion is Monday mornings and one or two additional mornings, as well as an afternoon or two. Perhaps it is:
  - Mondays from 8:30 – 10:00
  - Wednesdays from 8:30 – 10:30
  - Thursday from 2:30 – 4:30
  - Fridays from 8:30 – 10:00 and 3:00 – 4:30
- You might have to look a few weeks ahead to find the best slots to capture.
- When you block those times, create a new Category (Outlook) or Label (Gmail) and call it something that will help you keep that time for yourself. I've seen many creative Appointment Titles that my clients have come up with when doing this exercise:
  - Brainpower Hour
  - Deep Dive – Do Not Disturb
  - Get Sh*t Done Session
  - Distraction-Free Deep Work
  - Project Push Time
  - Laser Mode: ON
  - Creation Station
  - Clarity Block
- And my personal favorite:
  - Don't let Another Distraction Hijack Your Day, Sarah!!!!
- Make sure to set this appointment to recur, then save and close.

At this moment, you do not know what you will be working on during that block of time. And that's ok. The point is not to define what you will be doing (yet). The goal is to save that time for the Future You, so that when the day comes, you've given her a little gift she will appreciate. If you do have a Tetris-Style Calendar currently, just think about how grateful you'd be if you saw a large block of time on there today – already guarded and saved for you to play with. What would that feel like?

Maybe it would feel like tucking a $100 bill into the pocket of a winter coat at the end of the season. When you discover it months later, it feels like magic.

Or maybe it feels like buying a $2 lottery scratcher and winning $500 (that happened to me one time).

Or maybe it is that feeling when you look at your calendar, and there is nothing scheduled, and you get to do whatever it is you want or need to do without any additional commitments, distractions, or responsibilities. Feels pretty good, right?

That blank block on your calendar is a little time-rich surprise you've stashed away for your Future Self to unwrap exactly when she needs it most.

Whether you have an open day or a jammed-packed day full of meetings, it is important to consider the work you need to get done and commit the time and space on your calendar to do so. Which is why, together, we blocked some time on your calendar on a recurring basis.

That, of course, is the first step in order to achieve your goals, get more done, and feel accomplished at the end of each day and each week. Let's dig into the next steps for having a Perfectly Productive Workday.

Step 2. Invest in Changed Behavior

The next step in the Three-Step Process to the Perfectly Productive Workday is to use Deep Work time to get the work you know you need or want done, instead of giving that time away to someone else. Or instead of using that time to work on other things that will not move you forward with your goals or desired outcomes.

As you already know from experience, the Deep Work block alone on your calendar is not enough. It is often easy to see the white space (or even the Deep Work hold) on your calendar and find it hijacked or given away to others, or have a false and exaggerated idea of how much you'll be able to accomplish.

I know this because at times I have done it too. Doing that, giving that blocked time away, is almost always connected to unproductive behaviors that are triggered by either **internal challenges** or **external challenges**.

Let's address both of those areas of unproductive habits.

The Internal Challenges.

Humans are surprisingly uncomplicated beings, and yet, we overcomplicate a lot. When it comes to behavior, what you and I desire the most is to make it easy with a trigger, an action, and a reward.

- The **trigger** is any cue to take the action.
- The **action** is to do the thing.
- The **reward** is the immediate gratification for taking the action.

When faced with two immediate choices, we naturally want to pick the action that gets us to the reward faster.

Consider this scenario. It's 2:00 p.m. on a Saturday. You have been meaning to work out all day, and it hasn't happened yet. You're considering going to the gym now when a friend texts you and asks if you want to go out and grab a glass of wine together.

Which do you choose?

There are days you might choose the gym, but that likely does not come easily. Most often, you will probably decide that the glass of wine (or coffee) with a friend is the way to go. (I know from personal experience this often happens.)

Why?

The journey to the reward in the second option is immediate, tangible, and enjoyable. The **trigger** is your friend's invitation; the behavior is getting dressed and driving to meet her; and the reward is a glass of wine and social time.

The gym, on the other hand, the **trigger** to do that action is your own thought to go to the gym. Without external accountability and the ability to see and feel the reward, well, it isn't as strong.

The **behavior** is getting dressed and dragging yourself to the gym or wherever you work out, and the **reward** is not as tangible or immediate. Sure, you often feel better after you work out, but the true reward – losing weight, getting stronger, muscle toning – does not show up immediately. And, when faced with the decision, you can almost taste the reward of the wine, and remembering how good a workout feels when you're done is somehow erased each and every time.

To avoid rash, unproductive decisions in the moment, we need to set up appropriate cues and triggers. But, first, let's look at why, in the moment, we frequently pick the wrong things to work on – and beat ourselves up later for doing so.

Another Distraction Hijacked by Dopamine

You and I discussed earlier that we make 35,000 decisions every day. It's no wonder that when you have time to work on something, you often select what is easy and will immediately produce a reward or dopamine hit. But it's later in the day, when you audit the actions you've taken thus far in the day against your To-Do list, that you berate yourself for not working on what you should have worked on.

As we just discussed, it is not entirely your fault. Your simple brain wants a trigger, and it wants to mentally simulate a reward in order to take an action.

When faced with going to the gym at 2:00 p.m. or spending time with a friend, we most often choose the latter. A similar thing happens when you have the Deep Work time on your calendar. Having too many decisions about how to use that time is stressful. That stress causes analysis paralysis, which is the result of your prefrontal cortex trying to think clearly, your anterior cingulate flagging uncertainty, and your amygdala flaring up with stress — all at once.

That alone sounds stressful, doesn't it? The more stressed you are, the more the amygdala takes over, reducing access to the clear, rational thinking of the prefrontal cortex. You see how, without a simple cue or trigger, the action or behavior is not entirely your fault?

When your prefrontal cortex – the decision-making part of your brain - is hiding because it is in overload, then your brain looks for the easiest reward and the most immediate dopamine hit. This is why you have not used Deep Work time intentionally until now. Because, until now, you have not set yourself up to succeed.

Without the trigger and reward defined and evident, your brain will over-analyze or freeze. This leads to procrastination or delay in what you need to do.

From Procrastinator to Producer

If you think about our behavior when we are stressed and over-whelmed, we are often in fight-or-flight mode. This is the automatic physiological response triggered by the amygdala when the brain perceives a threat or high stress. And the freeze mode – not taking any action or taking actions that are not relevant to the important task at hand – is what we are doing when we are neither fighting nor flighting, but instead we are freezing.

Now, I don't know about you, but I have always called this procrastinating.

"I am procrastinating on starting that presentation outline."
"I am procrastinating on going to the grocery store or the gym."
"I am procrastinating on doing that research."

Joseph R. Ferrari, Ph.D., is a prominent psychologist and professor based at DePaul University in Chicago, known for his deep expertise in *chronic procrastination* and related decision-making behaviors. Dr. Ferrari explains that procrastination is not the same behavior as delaying. He says, *"If I am stuck on the tarmac and my plane isn't getting off, and I am four hours late for some appointment, then I didn't procrastinate. That's a delay."*

That makes sense, right?

For a moment, put yourself in that moment at work when you have two or more hours of open time on your calendar, a long list of things you need to do, and you're feeling stuck. You're feeling overwhelmed and stressed about it all. In that moment, at least from my experience, there is almost always a very clear task that needs to be done. And it is often the task I do not want to do.

Without setting up the right cue, which we will discuss, I find myself delaying that critical task and doing everything else on my list. I am lying to myself and saying I am being productive – because I am getting things done – but I am avoiding the one big task that is the thing I should be doing.

What Dr. Ferrari points out is that I am not a chronic procrastinator; I am procrastinating or delaying on this one task. But in general, I am not someone who chronically procrastinates on many things in my life.

You might be thinking, what is the difference between procrastinating and being a chronic procrastinator?
Dr. Ferrari says that everybody procrastinates, but not everyone is a procrastinator. Twenty percent of adult men and women are chronic procrastinators. That may not seem like a lot, but Dr. Ferrari points out that the percentage is higher than depression, substance abuse, panic attacks, and alcoholism. And unlike any of those diagnoses, we often associate procrastination with humor. Just open your favorite browser and type in "procrastination humor," and you will get a plethora of silly memes and graphics making fun of this common behavior.

If you procrastinate on a task, or repeatedly on the same task you dislike, you procrastinate.

If you procrastinate on many tasks and in different spaces and at different times, then you are a chronic procrastinator. For example, you are likely in the twenty percent of chronic procrastinators if you are someone who:

- Does not RSVP to events on time.
- Frequently run your gas tank to empty before you fill it up.

- Does not show up to events on time or at all because you failed to buy the tickets before they sold out.
- Receives a third and final bill or invoice before you finally pay it.

What do you think? Do you sometimes procrastinate or delay? Or are you a chronic procrastinator?

If you are a chronic procrastinator, I want to translate more of what Dr. Ferrari says. Before we dive in, the high-level take-away is 1) you learned to behave this way, so you can unlearn it, 2) you live in a society that supports being a procrastinator, and 3) you are not serving yourself or others around you in a healthy way.

As we have established, procrastination is a learned tendency, and cultural and societal expectations support it. Consider, for a minute, some of the examples Dr. Ferrari discusses in which our society encourages procrastination on getting things done.

Credit Card Payments. You will receive a penalty charge or interest if you pay late, but there is no reward for paying early each month.

Paying the IRS. If you owe, there is little benefit to paying earlier than April 15th. If you keep your money, you earn interest on it. The IRS does not discount for early payments.

Christmas Shopping. Often, discounts on items occur on Christmas Eve, which supports last-minute shopping. Additionally, return policies can affect your desire to buy early.

Hotel Stays. Companies like Hotel Tonight offer big discounts on hotel stays if you wait until the last minute to book them.

Entering your Billable Time. Many of my clients have to get their billable time entered on some regular cadence – and certainly by the end of the month. Often, the excitement of waiting until the last minute is the reward that the adrenaline junkies crave. You know it isn't best practice, yet each month you do it again and again and again.

Let's discuss why this behavior is not serving you, nor is it serving others.

Procrastination is the irrational and intentional delay of a target task, which prevents you from reaching your goals. The research shows that it is also a maladaptive lifestyle. Chronic procrastinators are often operating in *A World About Me* instead of what it should be – *A World About **We**.*

Research says that chronic procrastinators are very good excuse makers. They always have a reason that they couldn't get something done on time, or it took longer than expected, which is why it was late. Their reasons are logical, they often make sense, and they are often repeated over and over again. Because, as Dr. Ferrari points out, for the chronic procrastinator, they think that the world is all about me.

There are typically two things going on behind the chronic procrastination:

The blaming of time and the justification that you work better under pressure.

Chronic procrastinators are not lazy. In fact, they are often working their butts off on something. But there is something else that they should be working on – that thing that they are procrastinating on – and they often subconsciously (or maybe consciously at times) think:

> *"If I don't do that task or delay doing it, and I do something else productive and take my time doing that other thing, then I can say that I simply didn't have enough time."*

You've done that before, right? I know I have done that at times. And it usually doesn't feel good.

Or we use the delay to explain why the work product is not as great as what we know we are capable of.

> *"This is not my best work product. This is as good as it could be given the time I had to work on it. If only I had more time, I could have done better."*

We know that a lack of effort is not a positive image, but it is better than producing a piece of garbage.

I'm going to get real here for a minute. This happened to me while writing this book. I found myself delaying finishing the manuscript and turning it in to my editor. I found myself still productive and still "working on the book," but doing things that seemed productive but weren't.

During one meeting with my editor, I outlined for him the plan and timeline for the next steps on the book. In short, it was research, research, research; then self-edit and continue writing; then read through it; and then submit the final manuscript to the editor.

He stopped me and recommended that I switch my plan and timeline. He said to me,

> *"This is what you need to do: finish writing, submit it to me, and then you and I will together decide if it needs more writing or more research inserted."*

In this moment, I explained to my editor,

> *"I do not consider myself a procrastinator, and I have every intention to get the book published, but I now know what I am doing. I am avoiding finishing the book.*

You see, right now, as I write it, I am getting all of the accolades for writing it. People are impressed that I am writing a book; they are asking about the book, they are talking about the book. And, I don't even have to finish the book in order to absorb all of the rewards of being an author and publishing a book.

What if I finish it and it sucks? It is garbage. Nobody likes it! I'd rather be "writing a book" and continue to reap those benefits than to finish the book, and it sucks."

The lack of effort is not great, but it is better than being done and having a crappy book.

Side Note: Here is where I can't help but experience a moment of curiosity and hope that you like this book. But you know what, I am completely okay with whatever your opinion of the book is. You have a right to your opinion, and if that means it isn't your favorite read, then that is ok. There isn't a book that exists that every reader thinks is incredible. If you do like or love the book, take a moment to review it on Amazon or Goodreads. If you don't like it, well, then maybe consider delaying or procrastinating on writing your review. My 5-star rating will appreciate your procrastinating tendencies. I'm kidding, of course.

Anyway, if the blaming of time or the last-minute adrenaline rush gets you moving and focused, then let's discuss what you can do to overcome procrastination and prioritize working on that important task when the time and space allow for it.

You were not born a procrastinator; you learned to behave that way, and you can unlearn it. Procrastinators also often think that they are the exception. They think, "*This is all interesting, but…some of my best work happens when I am under pressure.*"

A common misconception is that people work better under pressure, but research shows that stress actually impairs cognitive function, reduces creativity, and increases the likelihood of mistakes. The perceived productivity often comes from adrenaline-fueled urgency, not from doing higher-quality work.

Experiments have been conducted worldwide in which participants are asked how they performed on tasks under pressure. Many believed they did great, and their work product was fantastic. Most, however, made more errors when their last-minute work product was reviewed.

James Clear, author of *Atomic Habits*, is widely recognized for translating behavioral science into practical, actionable strategies for building better habits and improving daily life. Along similar lines, Cal Newport, author of *Slow Productivity*, emphasizes the importance of working at a sustainable pace rather than constantly rushing. Newport writes,

> *"There are boring physiological and neurological explanations for this effect involving the mind-constricting impacts of cortisol when your schedule becomes unrealistically full, or the time required to excite rich semantic connections among your brain's neurons. But we don't need science to convince us of something that we've all experienced directly: our brains work better when we're not rushing."*

As Newport suggests, there is extensive scientific research supporting the idea that we function better when we avoid constant rushing or last-minute pressure, but most of us have already experienced this truth firsthand.

In fact, recently, my client Rebecca was pleased to update me about a report that she had to prepare. During our session the prior week, we spoke about what she was currently procrastinating on – that report, of course. We broke down the steps to finalize it and send it to her partner, before delivering it to the client.

When we reflected on the prior week, Rebecca was thrilled to report that she got it done on the timeline we outlined – and that the partner said it was very well done and had no edits to it.

Rebecca said that in the past, this partner would often have a lot of edits, and Rebecca said it was 100% because she would wait until the last minute to do it, knowing that it would not be her best work. And, here's the catch, when Rebecca is rushing and waiting until the last minute, she makes more mistakes, and she yields a poorer deliverable. And, in that situation, the recipient (in this case, her partner) is also reviewing it in a heightened state-of-mind, which means that person is more inclined to identify more mistakes and issues or feel more frustrated by the work product. It's a catch-22.

Like Rebecca, you are not an exception to what the research shows. You think you work better under pressure, but your work quality suffers, you experience more stress, you are less creative, and you make both minor and significant mistakes.

So, how do you change?

How do you mitigate procrastination and get more done in a timely manner?

The Premack Effect, proposed by psychologist David Premack, states that a more desirable or high-probability behavior can be used as a reward to reinforce a less desirable or low-probability behavior.

In simple terms, *you can increase motivation by letting yourself do something you enjoy only after completing something you're less motivated to do.*

For example, you can watch Netflix after you finish your report. Or you can eat that piece of chocolate after you spend twenty-five minutes working on this research.

You can drink from your Perfectly Productive Day mug only after you've already spent time invested in your Perfectly Productive Morning.

Consider, for a minute, something you need to work on. What is it? Have you identified it?

Great. Now, what is something you need to do that you like doing? Got it?

Great, now use the Premack Effect to tie those activities together. Can you say to yourself, *"I will get my billable time entered for last week. Every time I submit an entry, I will take a sip of my latte."*

Remember – we are simple creatures at the end of all of this. We need a **trigger**, an **action**, and a **reward**. You are over-complicating the trigger by procrastinating and delaying the action. Instead, consider how to trick your brain and associate the action with a different reward. In this case, we know what the task is, and we are associating the action of entering the billable time with an immediate reward of taking a sip of our latte. You can only take a sip of your latte when you successfully submit a time entry (or an entire day – your choice).

Additionally, science repeatedly proves that external account-ability works. Consider using social media, a trusted colleague, or your entire team as a tool for overcoming procrastination.

> *"I need to spend my Deep Work time this morning working on preparing for the big client meeting on Thursday. I will have the outline submitted to you by noon."*

I would also encourage you to challenge cultural and societal norms. Consider the earlier examples of how our society promotes procrastination. Dr. Ferrari explained that he always pays his bills as soon as he receives them. Instead of waiting to pay it, since there is no reward for paying early, he chooses to pay immediately so he can be done with it. That's a reward in and of itself!

This is usually how I handle paying bills and booking things as well. It is liberating and freeing to just get it done. And, you can often schedule credit card and IRS payments for a future date. When I receive the bill on July 10th, I immediately allocate the charges and schedule the payment for around the date it is due. This way, I can manage the entire process in one sitting without having to think about it. I also do not incur a penalty charge for being late.

- Get your billable time entered contemporaneously.
- Finish that report and submit it to your boss thirty minutes before you said you would.
- Prepare for Friday's client meeting on Tuesday.
- Schedule next month's conference trip now.

Here is my promise to you. Despite what you have previously told yourself, completing the task is a better image than the lack of effort, blaming time, and finishing things at the eleventh hour. Others don't take your late work positively, no matter how amazing it is. They appreciate and respect your ability to manage your time and deliver as expected.

Over time, if you change this behavior, you, too, will see that there is an amazing feeling of getting things done ahead of schedule. I believe in you, and I believe you can control these internal challenges that we've discussed.

Now, let's explore those external challenges that can get in the way of working on the identified tasks during the scheduled Deep Work time.

The External Challenges.

Let's remind ourselves of the scene at the start of our Perfectly Productive Workday on Tuesday, April 2nd. We've just arrived at my Shoffice. It's 7:00 a.m., and we have blocked time until 8:30 a.m. for Deep Work. This is ninety minutes of work time you get to use to play with and prioritize what to get done.

We have already discussed some of the internal challenges that get in the way of working on the top project or task. Now, it's time to explore the external challenges – the seemingly more difficult to control interrupters. Let's start with interruptions and distractions.

Reclaim the Control You Didn't Know You Had

I know you because at times I am you. We have the best of intentions at 7:00 a.m., and yet we allow all of the interruptions, distractions, and inefficient multitasking to take over…. and then we blame them, and we beat ourselves up, too.

Why didn't you get that research done this morning? You ask yourself.

Because I had too many emails to respond to.

Why didn't you finish the client report during your afternoon block? You question.

Right after my lunch meeting, news broke out about a theft in my neighborhood, and it was all over my social media feed.

Why didn't you make progress on the article you're writing? You consider.

Because Jane asked to meet with me and it was the only time we both had available this morning.

Do these all sound familiar? A signature presentation that I offer is ***Stop Welcoming the Distractions***. During this engaging and insightful program, I ask the audience to reflect on their biggest distractions and interruptions. What are yours? Think about them and pause here for a moment to note them in the Perfectly Productive Day Workbook.

Did you note some of these:

- Email
- Phone Calls
- Text Messages
- Slack or other Instant Messages
- People Stopping by your Office / Desk
- Social Media
- Meetings
- Surprise Meetings / Appointments
- Emergencies
- Other People Talking / Chatter
- Getting Stuck on a Project
- Computer or System Issues
- Getting Sucked into a Rabbit Hole (e.g,. during research)

I am sure you resonate with a lot of these and more! Even procrastination and analysis paralysis are technically distractions or interruptions.

During my presentation, I introduced the concept that there is a distinction between distractions and interruptions.

Distractions can appear internally or externally, and they are often clearly *within* your control.

Interruptions, on the other hand, are external and are often *not within* your control.

If you were to separate this list to fit nicely into one of these two categories, you might note the list of these External Challenges like this:

Distractions (Internal or External and Within Your Control):

- Social Media
- Getting Stuck on a Project
- Getting Sucked into a Rabbit Hole (e.g., during research)
- Procrastination
- Analysis Paralysis

Interruptions (External and Not Within Your Control):

- Email
- Phone Calls
- Text Messages
- Slack or other Instant Messages
- People Stopping By Office/Desk
- Meetings
- Surprise Meetings / Appointments
- Emergencies
- Other People Talking / Chatter

Is that how you would separate them, or something similar? Here is how I would separate them:

Distractions (Internal or External and Within Your Control):

- Email
- Phone Calls
- Text Messages
- Slack or other Instant Messages
- People Stopping By Office/Desk
- Social Media
- Meetings
- Surprise Meetings / Appointments
- Emergencies
- Other People Talking / Chatter
- Getting Stuck on a Project
- Computer or System Issues
- Getting Sucked into a Rabbit Hole (e.g., during research)
- Procrastination
- Analysis Paralysis

Interruptions (External and Not Within Your Control):

- Phone Calls
- Meetings
- Emergencies
- Other People Talking / Chatter
- Getting Stuck on a Project
- Computer or System Issues

Notice that most of the events that stayed listed under Interruptions are also listed as Distractions. This is because,

I would argue, most seemingly uncontrollable interruptions, with few exceptions, are really distractions in disguise.

Let's break down a few of them that you might be questioning right now.

Email is often considered to be an interruption, and you may have noticed that I noted it as a distraction only. *But email interrupts me all day long*, you might be thinking.

Ask yourself this question: *What, if anything, could I do to control email from interrupting me when I am trying to work on this important project?*

Did you come up with something?

If you really consider that question, *What could I do to control email from interrupting me?* – You probably came up with an idea or two.

I could turn off notifications.

I could shut down email while I am working on that project.

I could use a separate computer that does not have access to my email or the internet.

I could let my team know I am unavailable for the next few hours as I focus on the big client report.

Are you starting to see and believe that there are many options for how you could control that distraction?

Let's take another one. Let's explore Emergencies since I left that one on both the Interruption and Distraction lists.

Emergencies in the workplace do occur, and sometimes they are truly uncontrollable, or they are a one-time event. In those situations, we would consider it an interruption – it was external and not much you could do about it.

There are, however, many instances where emergencies occur, and they shouldn't have happened. Or they are the definition of insanity – repeating the same thing over and over. An example of this would be a recurring project or task that always seems to surprise you and is considered an emergency.

Many of my clients generate invoices each month to review and then send them to clients. Often, their accounting team has a process each month wherein they generate invoices, and a billing lead has to review them and get them turned back into accounting with mark-ups by a certain date.

Somehow, this event always seems to be a surprise and an emergency. Meetings are cancelled, emails go unanswered, or late-night working sessions are happening to fit in the time to review the invoices and turn them around in a timely manner.

What, if anything, could I do to control this interruption?

You might be thinking: nothing. There is nothing I can do. I just have to get them done.

You're right – you do just have to get them done. But you are creating a frenzied state of mind by not asking the question: *What, if anything, could I be doing to control this interruption?*

Did you think of an answer? I did.

You could block time on your calendar around the 1st of each month – or whatever day this project occurs typically – for the true length of time it takes to do it. That's what my client, Heather, does, and it is very effective to see and know that time is accounted for.

You could delegate a piece of the process to another team member. Ask them to take the first step in reviewing the documents and then submit them to you.

You could request pieces of the project early. For example, if we are talking about reviewing invoices at the start of each month, maybe you have a client or two that you haven't done any more work for since the 10th of the prior month. Request that their pre-bill be generated earlier in the month for review to reduce the volume of reviews you need to complete.

The point is, you can be very creative and find ways to control even the biggest interruptions in your life if you just ask the important question:

What, if anything, could I do to control this interruption?

Another thing that shows up on both lists is computer, system, and IT issues. These, of course, happen and are extremely frustrating. There is a wide range in the types of computer or IT issues we face and in how much control we have over them. This is why I listed these as interruptions rather than distractions.

I am a small business, and up until a few years ago, I acted as my company's IT department as well. When something went wrong on the computer – and believe me, it would – then that event would interrupt my flow, and I'd have to turn into the CTO of my company (Chief Technology Officer). Many productive hours were lost to dealing with my computer and IT issues. So frustrating!

Eventually, the pain point became too large, and I asked myself: *What, if anything, could I do to control the computer issues from happening to me and wasting that precious time?*

I hired an external MSP (Managed Service Provider). Now, when it is a computer or systems issue, I just book a time with my MSP, and they troubleshoot the issue for me.

When working from home, the internet is sometimes the IT issue. As I am sure you can relate to, that is sometimes so frustrating. You are in a meeting, working on a document, or reviewing email when the internet becomes spotty or goes out entirely. Grrrrr.

What, if anything, could I do to control this interruption?

When it is a temporary issue, like there is just an outage or spotty connection, I often have a backup plan of where I can go to get reliable internet to continue focusing. On some occasions, I pack up my computer and the work I need to do, then drive to a nearby coffee shop to stay focused.

When it was a bigger issue, as when I had chronic internet connectivity problems, I ran a temporary Cat5 cable from the back of my router into my computer. Once I knew that solved the Wi-Fi connectivity problems, I hired an electrician to run the wire along the roofline and into my Shoffice.

You see, with most interruptions, there is something that you could have or should have done to control them. *What is it?*

What, if anything, could you do to control that interruption?

You are smart, and I am confident that you will come up with something. And remember, it isn't that you are being selfish or rude. You are considering the work you need to focus on to serve your team, your clients, and your colleagues.

Whenever you are faced with an interruption, ask yourself the critical question, stop and consider your options to control it, and demand back your day. Now, let's set some boundaries to ensure your blocked time remains within your control.

The Architecture of Time: Build Your Bridges

In 2022, I was booked to speak at an industry conference in Austin, Texas. The conference co-chairs and I were at a virtual pre-conference interview and consultation about the contents of my program, From *Chaos* to **Control.**

"Your program sounds great," one of them said.

The other chimed in with, "*Please tell me that you do not use the word* **boundaries** *in your presentation. Ugh. I hate that word. My teenage daughter and her friends use it all of the time, and it has no meaning anymore.*"

I jotted down a note in that moment: "*note to self — do not use the word* **boundaries** *in the presentation.*"

Do you also get a visceral reaction to that word? I don't, but I recognize that some people do.

Being extra aware of this, I've been careful about when and how I use the word. And then I heard a quote from Trent Shelton, former NFL player and motivational speaker,

Wow. Powerful. Boundaries are bridges to let the right things and people in.

With that in mind, where in your life and in your day do you need to build bridges and create some boundaries?

You may need to set boundaries around your emotional well-being, money, habits, mental health, and time.

You and I are focused mostly on the latter – your time – but it can also directly impact these other areas.

Boundaries are also tricky because they are, arguably, an internal challenge that is disguised as an external challenge. At their core, boundaries are about self-respect and making intentional choices that align with our priorities and needs.

If you allow other people to hijack or claim your time, they will always take it. If you give someone an inch, they will take a mile.

Your boundaries have to be clearly communicated to others. Now, I am not saying that, in response to someone's asking for your time, you need to shout: "*No, I have boundaries, and you are violating them!*"

Often, your boundaries are communicated without ever using that word, or even without saying a word. In fact, our discussion of distractions and interruptions is really about how you can identify, define, and enforce your boundaries.

If you consider what needs boundaries when it comes to protecting your time, many of the things that you'd think of are meetings, people interrupting you, emails, people stopping by your office, phone calls, and instant messages – to name a few.

Typically, boundaries are needed when we recognize we have allowed these external things to monopolize our time or interrupt us too often. When we ask ourselves the important question – *What, if anything, could we do to control this interruption?* – What we are really doing is identifying and defining the thing that we need a boundary around. The last step – executing on your boundaries – is really about taking the action that you need to take in response to that critical question.

For example, you have identified that people coming by your office or desk is a major interruption in your workday. Up until this point, you've mostly thought that there isn't much to do about it.

You've now asked yourself that critical question:

**_What, if anything, could I do to
control this interruption?_**

You got creative and put a whiteboard on your desk credenza to let others know whether you are Available or in Focused Mode. This is now an example of you identifying, defining, and executing boundaries around others who chronically interrupt you.

Recently, I met someone at a virtual networking meeting. I reached out to her and invited her to a one-on-one meeting to get to know each other better. Within twenty-four hours, she responded to my invitation to connect, and she wrote:

> *"It was great talking with you. I apologize, but right now I'm taking a pause from one-on-one meetings to focus on client projects."*

She didn't block me or put up a wall. She built a bridge. She could have ignored my invitation or email. Chances are, I will forget I even sent it. Or she could engineer a bridge. Which, in my opinion, is what she did.

Her response was short, friendly, and honest. And I really appreciated it. In fact, I saved it. Even I can learn how to build better bridges when it comes to invitations to connect that I do not have time for right now.

Remember, boundaries are not walls; they are bridges. In the journey of our workday, we get so much farther when we build bridges around us.

Boundaries transition our frequent hijacking challenges into a beautiful bridge that we can define and control.

Turning Challenges into Controlled Choices

Did you notice a pattern with the External Challenges that we discussed? Did you notice how most of them can be controlled as well? In other words, even External Challenges are often Internal Challenges, wherein these events often occur because you haven't changed your behavior, expectations, boundaries, and communication to align with guarding your valuable time.

Let's get a little selfish and prioritize what you need to get done. But to be fair and candid, it really isn't selfish. Most of our work isn't about having a finished product that you keep only for yourself. Most of the work we need to get done is ultimately a deliverable for someone else: our team, our clients, or our bosses.

So, using your valuable Deep Work time to work on these deliverables is not selfish; it's smart. This is why your selfishness in guarding your valuable Deep Work time is essential to serve yourself and everyone else you are working with and for.

Now that we've identified the Internal and External Challenges that can derail your Deep Work time, let's explore the third and final step to your Perfectly Productive Workday.

Step 3. The System is the Solution

Alright, let's align here. You and I are discussing the Three-Step Process to The Perfectly Productive Workday.

Step One is to ensure you have the space and time on your calendar by blocking the Deep Work time. (If you still have not done that, I recommend you pause right now and block recurring time on your calendar. I actually just double-checked that I have Thursdays blocked because that is my current preferred Deep Work day.)

In **Step Two**, we covered the External and Internal Challenges to completing the work.

Now, we will explore **Step Three,** which is to identify what to work on. There are two critical components to this step. The first is having your To-Dos organized in a single place; the second is the skill to identify the priorities.

At this point, you've done everything right. You have blocked the Deep Work time on your calendar, and you've invested in yourself to identify your internal and external challenges. Now, you're ready to pick up that important project and start working on it.

Then, you start to spin. What is the most important thing to do right now? Was it emailed to me? Did I leave it on my notepad at home? Is it that proposal that woke me up last night?

This rumination is often caused by not having all of your projects, tasks, ideas, and To-Dos in a single Trusted System. From there, you can more easily prioritize what your focus should be during your Deep Work time. Let's dive deeper into those two components.

Before You Prioritize, Organize

The example above is all too common — our tasks are scattered across multiple places: three, four, fifteen, or more. Then, when we finally have time in our schedule to start working, we often waste it debating what to tackle first or, worse, reorganizing our To-Do list. That can leave us feeling productive, even though we haven't actually made progress on the work that matters.

This is why the organization and prioritization of your action items – your To-Do list – needs to happen before we arrive at the designated Deep Work time. It also needs to move from a To-Do list item – *Organize my To-Do List* – to just part of your daily work hygiene of keeping it updated and accurate.

A Trusted System is two parts. First, it is the place that you designated to write down and track your actionable items – your projects, tasks, To-Dos, and ideas – and, second, it is your system or method for getting those actionable items into that place. We'll dive deeper into both.

A Trusted System, once it is fully established and working effectively, is a dedicated space to store, update, and brain dump everything you need to do. This practice helps to mitigate distractions, interruptions, multitasking, and procrastination. It also helps you prioritize effectively and target the right thing to work on.

What are examples of Trusted Systems?

I am so glad you asked. There are thousands and thousands of project management software available on the market today. They each offer different functionality and user preferences. To give you an idea, some of the more common project management software include: Asana, Trello, Monday.com, Todoist, Wrike, Microsoft Planner, Airtable, ClickUp, and Jira.

Any of those programs can be and are Trusted Systems. Before I lose you to overwhelm, I wanted to assure you that the best Trusted System is the one that you will use.

In that case, a Trusted System *could be* pen and paper. There are some disadvantages to using pen and paper because the ability to recalibrate your To-Do list is limited, but it is an option. I have successfully helped my clients use this method to still track their important To-Dos and get them done during their Deep Work time.

Also, recognize that any and all of the digital Trusted Systems noted above are quite effective for project and task management. None of them is going to be perfect for you, because you are not the engineer who designed them. However, they are all perfectly perfect for what you need to track your important To-Dos and accomplish more. If you're ready to invest in one and you aren't sure where to start, check out the complimentary resource at www.perfectlypro-ductiveday.com/resources.

Once you've identified the Trusted System that is going to work best for you, use one of your Deep Work blocked times to gather all of your To-Dos and input them into the Trusted System.

Think about the emails, the different To-Do lists, the sticky notes at the bottom of your purse or laptop bag, the random sheets of paper, and those tasks left inside your brain. Also, don't forget about that important To-Do that you wrote down in the journal this morning – that thing that woke you up last night and you and I discussed bringing it with you today to your Perfectly Productive Workday.

Gather all of those random To-Dos and put them into the Trusted System. Even better, ask your assistant to put them in there for you. There is nothing to be embarrassed about – they already know your To-Do list lives in fifteen different locations, so they will be thrilled to help you get more organized.

Now that you have all of your projects, tasks, ideas, and To-Dos in a single Trusted System, the most important thing is to use it.

Make it a daily practice to open the Trusted System every day. Even if you have to set a calendar reminder for yourself while you build this new habit. Remember…*Productive people are productive because they use tools and systems to keep them on track.*

Build the habit of opening your Trusted System every morning as part of the systems that you launch each day in your browser on your computer. We are a species who want things at our ready now. When we think of a question, we need to be able to find the answer in just a few clicks. We need things to be easy and accessible at all times. When your Trusted System is not open, it feels like an extra step to get there to add new tasks. By opening it first thing in the morning as part of your setup routine, you have removed a few detours from your journey to success. Note: I've customized my default browser to automatically open a few websites I use daily, which helps me maintain my perfectly productive habits. One of those websites is my Trusted System site.

As you receive new To-Dos throughout the day – via email, your own thoughts, a meeting, or phone calls – add them to the Trusted System instead of a random sticky note. A simple hack for this is to write on the top sticky note:

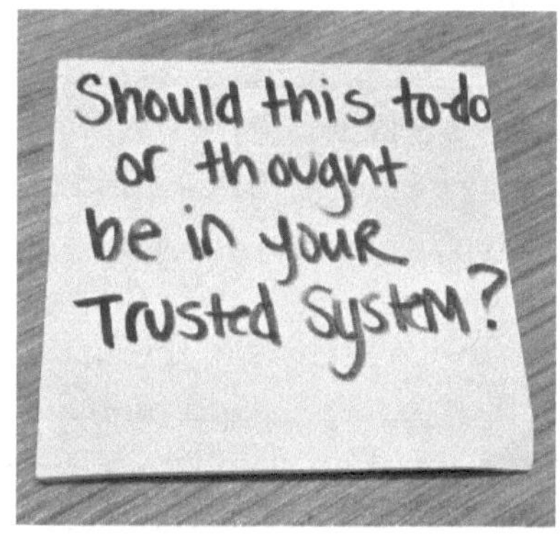

This way, when your old habit of grabbing the Post-It pad surfaces, this little note will remind you that you're building new habits.

Customize the location of this reminder. *Should this To-Do or thought be in your Trusted System?* By placing it wherever you historically would write your action items, whether that is in your notebook, on your laptop, or wherever you often jot down random thoughts and To-Dos. This way, that simple little note will be your coach reminding you of the new habits you are working hard to develop. Maybe add a smiley face or a sticker to it to reinforce that you're doing a good job. Remember, habits are formed by a trigger (the note), an action (putting it into the new Trusted System), and a **reward** (the amazing feeling of being organized and getting the intentional things done each day).

Now, let's address how to identify the priorities or the intentional things that you need to do.

Your Inner CEO Already Picked the Priority

My signature program is called From *Frazzled* to **Focused**. During that program, we address multitasking, brain dumping into a Trusted System, and then how to take those skills and design an intentional workday. It is an engaging, informative, and fun program that has helped many professionals with their time management, organization, and productivity.

Often during the Q&A portion of the program, a professional will ask me what the best method is for prioritizing their daunting and never-ending To-Do list or Trusted System. You can probably relate. Because we all have a To-Do list that is the length of the book, *War and Peace* (which is just under 1300 pages long). I put this here so you don't stop reading this book in search of how long that book really is – and that's a good thing.

Imagine having a career where you had to just show up and wait for someone to tell you what to do. How draining and boring that would be, right? You're reading this book because you are someone who is successful and driven and wants to accomplish a lot in your life. Having the choice to prioritize is a great thing!

And here is some great news. You already know what to do, and so I am just going to remind you.

There is not one single magic answer to prioritizing. Once, I heard someone say that there is no such thing as a C priority because you only ever work on A priorities. And I agree with that statement.

I don't think I have ever lived a day where I have identified my A, B, and C priorities and I've worked my way through them all. Nope. Usually, I barely get through my A priority list – and then I recalibrate for the next day or the next Deep Work block. That is when and how C-priority projects work their way up to A-priority status.

Not everything can be an A-level priority right now — if everything on your To-Do list were the highest priority, then nothing would truly be a priority at all. You have to identify what the A1, the A2, and the A3 priorities are and work in order of those and recalibrate after. Without identifying your A priority, you will always be working on the B to Z priorities, and B to Z priorities are literally just keeping you busy (get it, busy – B-Z).

So, how do you do that? What are some of the things to consider when identifying what your priorities need to be right now? Let's explore that together, and again, I am just reminding you of these because I know you're smart, and most of these you already know.

Prioritize the Upcoming Deadline. First, what project is tied to the upcoming deadline? Sometimes, we cannot escape the fact that the number one project right now is the one that is due today or that we promised to someone. I hate these priorities because the extra pressure of the deadline approaching creates stress and an uncomfortable pressure in my body. Those are the days when I feel like I got something done during my Deep Work block, but I still don't feel in control at the end of the day. I don't feel satisfied that I worked on my To-Do list and intentions, and instead feel as though I just met a deadline. Try to avoid these last-minute rushes when possible. Which is why we want to prioritize using the other criteria as often as possible and not defining our A1 because it is what is most urgent. Having a Trusted System and boundaries – remember, we discussed those earlier – will help with this.

Clear Bottlenecks for Others. Another method to prioritize is to consider what you need to do that will unlock bottlenecks for others on your team. Sometimes a project that is not high on your priority list needs to move from a C priority to an A priority so that, when it becomes your A priority, the pre-work on it has already been done. This is the art of effective delegation.

Address What's on Your Mind. Sometimes the priority is whatever is keeping you up at night or taking up mental headspace in this moment. Often, when I am faced with multiple priorities, I will just close my eyes and pay attention to my thoughts. Taking a minute to watch them fly by, and eventually the one that needs my attention today will stand out. That thought or To-Do then becomes my biggest priority and I focus my efforts on just that.

Clear the Decks. During the scheduled Deep Work blocks, I recommend working on a project – something that requires longer blocks of time to focus and execute. However, there are certainly days when my Deep Work block needs to be used to clear the decks. That might mean reviewing emails, spending time on a bunch of smaller tasks that need to get done, or maybe finally calling customer support on that insurance claim and recognizing that you might be on hold for hours. When those activities pile up and start to collectively carry the weight of a bag of bricks, I realign my priority list with clearing the decks so I can focus on a critical project during my next Deep Work session.

Commit to Your Choice. And finally, here is the golden ticket. The magic key to prioritizing is to be confident in what you selected to work on. Too much of your time is wasted picking the A1 priority and then changing your mind. This happens because, while working on the A1 priority, you are distracted by an email from someone who claims they need you to do something immediately. And you believe them, you believe that you should be working on that thing, instead of holding true to yourself and being confident in the A1 project that you selected to work on.

Or you are working on an A1 priority and then remember or are reminded of the A3 priority. Then you doubt yourself and your original decision to work on the A1 priority, and you switch tasks and start working on the A3 priority.

This behavior, also known as frequent multitasking, leads to leaked time and frequently not finishing important tasks. What is even worse than that is that this behavior is further convincing you that you are not trustworthy. You are training yourself to say that you can't be trusted to select the priority because you might be wrong. This is not healthy or productive. Remember in the Morning Routine, we talked about trusting ourselves when Dr. Chatterjee said it was one of the main objectives for his daily five-minute workout habit – to show that he can rely on himself, and he trusts himself.

Trust yourself. You picked that top priority project for a reason. Choose your A1 priority and stick with it until it is done – or at the appropriate stopping point for that Deep Work block of time.

You already know most of this, but having it validated helps you see that you are capable of prioritizing effectively. The A2 priority will come faster if you stay the course and finish the A1 priority. The A3 priority will move up the list, and you will reach the C2 priority once it becomes the A1, thanks to the prioritization skills we discussed.

You got this.

Let's briefly recap. Prioritization means reviewing your To-Dos and assessing:

- What projects have upcoming deadlines?
- What projects would unlock bottlenecks and help others get started?
- What is taking up mental headspace for me, and I just need to get it done?
- What are the small tasks that can be easily checked off to clear my head and stress?
- What is the one thing I've decided to do that I just need to get started on and stay committed to?

Prioritization isn't about finding the perfect answer — it's about making a thoughtful decision, honoring it, and proving to yourself that you can be trusted to follow through. We discussed earlier that identifying the priority should be made before you sit down during that Deep Work block of time. Let's explore when and how to do that.

CHAPTER 9

Navigating the Realities of Work

et's go back to the start of our Perfectly Productive Workday together. At 7:00 a.m., once inside my Shoffice, you and I are greeted by a rolling cart next to my clear desk. On top of the cart is the roadmap for how to approach my day. This architectural design of my day does not magically appear. It takes thoughtful consideration and planning the day before.

For a minute, imagine it is 1995, and you are about to take off on a journey from Los Angeles to Canada. What do you do first?

Remember, it's 1995, so GPS on your phone does not work. You're anxious to get driving, but you are smart enough to realize you can't just get behind the wheel and start driving.

You'd likely first prepare a plan for how you'll get there. You would likely map out the entire journey, highlighting the routes you need or want to take on your foldable interstate and highway maps. At the very least, you would highlight the route you aimed to take for the day's journey. (Oh, and the 2000's version of the foldable maps was printing out a detailed map from MapQuest.)

Michael Watkins is the author of *The First 90 Days*, a book about accelerating leadership transitions through strategy, relationships, and early wins. Michael says,

> *"Ultimately, success or failure emerges from the accumulation of daily choices that propel you in productive directions or push you off a cliff...you need to be more disciplined about planning.*
>
> *At the end of each day, spend ten minutes evaluating how well you met your goals and then planning for the next day. Do the same thing at the end of each week. Get into the habit of doing this. Even if you fall behind, you will be more in control."*

The point is, you would do a little planning rather than just setting out on your adventure. When it comes to your Perfectly Productive Workday, it's often too easy to just "show up to work" and get things done. But without a plan, it is like taking off on a road trip eight hours away without using a map of any kind. "I'm just going to jump in the car and head in the general direction that I am supposed to go and hope for the best."

That would be absurd, and you would end up driving off a cliff. Let's keep you on the road and on track to arrive safely, productively, and relaxing to your favorite road trip tunes.

The Shut Down Routine is essentially doing just that – it's leaving the roadmap of your day on your desk so that when you arrive – coffee in hand, fully charged and fueled up, ready to accelerate and go – you already know the journey of your day.

So, let's rewind back for a moment to my workday yesterday, on Monday, April 1st, and what I did so that today my architectural roadmap of my day is ready to support me on this Perfectly Productive Workday of Tuesday, April 2nd.

The Shut Down Routine is something that I recommend doing toward the end of the workday, but not at the very end of the workday. Let's say you plan on stopping work at 5:00 p.m. In that case, you would not plan to do the Shut Down Routine at 4:50 p.m.

You would complete it around 3:00 p.m. The Shut Down Routine should be done two to three hours before your workday ends. It isn't complicated, but it does require some discipline to build the habit of doing it daily. Many clients I have worked with have reported the benefits of this daily practice, even after initially feeling a resistance to trying it.

So, what is the Shut Down Routine?

I'm glad you asked. Let's discuss it.

It's 3:00 p.m., and you just finished a meeting. You have another meeting at 4:00 p.m. and plan on leaving work around 5:00 p.m. Your To-Do list seems endless, and the emails keep flooding in. It seems the most productive thing to do is just keep getting things done and checking off the list. Pause. Breathe. Stop. It's time to do the Shut Down Routine before diving into that next task.

Grab a blank sheet of paper, a journal, or a tablet. The tool does not matter; however, I do recommend you write it down (versus typing it out). There's robust scientific research showing that writing things down improves retention, largely because it engages your brain in deeper cognitive processing.

Tara Donohue Rudo owns No More Piles, a professional organizing business in Baltimore, Maryland. She says that she *"writes out my office day To-Dos on paper since it helps me stay on track."*

Ready to write? Ok, here is what you do for the Shut Down Routine:

1. **Review The Day.**
   - What is on the calendar for tomorrow?
   - What are the non-negotiables (meetings, phone calls, appointments, travel, sports activities for the kids)?

2. **Consider the Preparation and Follow-Up Needed.**
   - For any meetings, appointments, etc. on the calendar, do you need any time to prepare?
   - Will there be any immediate follow-up that you will likely need to do? Hint: If it is a meeting, the answer is almost always YES. Even if the immediate follow-up is just reviewing your notes from the meeting, extracting anything you need to do, and putting it in your Trusted System. More on that later.
   - Equipped with this knowledge now (at 3:00 p.m. on the prior day), when will you get the Prep done? Tomorrow morning? This afternoon?

3. **Find and Define the Open Time.**
   - Once you've identified the non-negotiables, including their respective prep and follow-up, what is left is the Open Time (or blocked Deep Work time).
   - This is the time to get other work done and crossed off your To-Do list. How much time remains after Steps 1 and 2?
   - In that Open Time for tomorrow, prioritize and define what you will get done.

This three-step process is not just regurgitating your day on paper. It is about really thinking about what it will **look** and **feel** like to be you tomorrow. Here is a sample of what my Shut Down Routine might look like on any given day:

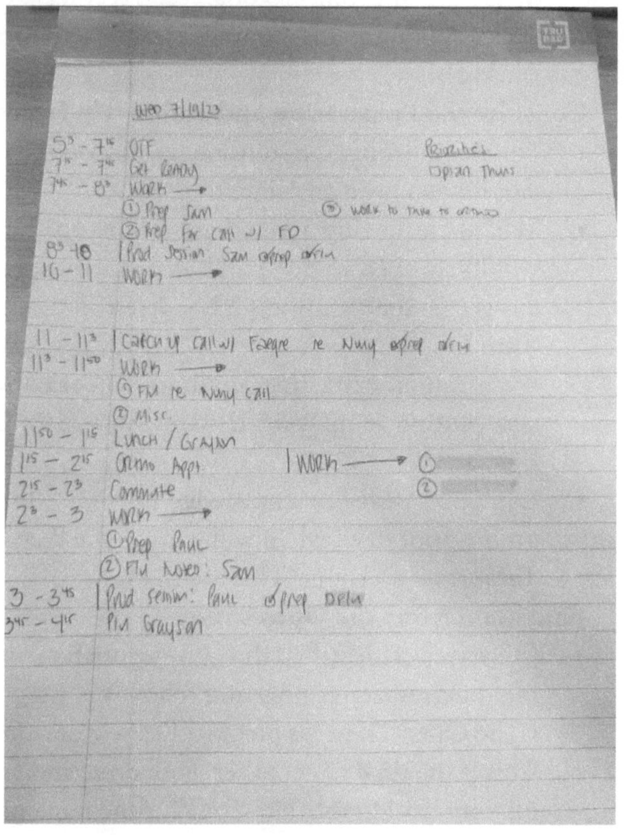

Maryann Reyes is Tax Principal at Withum in New Jersey, and she says,

"I like to keep track of the things that need my attention immediately - I like the "to-do list" that

way I can prioritize what needs to be done and feel accomplished when I cross it off. I also like to regroup at the end of the day to be prepared for tomorrow."

This is Maryann's way of completing a Shut Down Routine. My recommendation is to do this planning on the workday before so that you are ready to execute in the morning. However, if your Perfectly Productive Workday did not go as planned yesterday, you could always do it in the morning – before you ever check email, or else the plan will never occur.

Anne Sharp, a professional organizer whom you met earlier in our Perfectly Productive Morning, says,

> *"I primarily use a paper calendar and like the 3-tier funnel down system of the Planner Pad.*
>
> *At the start of the week, I write my weekly to-do's in the top section. At the start of each day, I review and update my day-specific to-do's in the middle section, and my time-specific to-do's in the bottom section.*
>
> *There is something cathartic about 'freeing your brain' of all those thoughts and writing them down. Then I get to check them off, which I love!"*

Even if we have our To-Do's in a digital productivity system, when it comes to the Shut Down Routine, it is incredibly powerful and effective to rewrite your top priorities with a pen and on paper.

Laura Leist is an organizing and productivity consultant and speaker, based in Redmond, Washington. She, too, agrees that writing down the current priorities is highly effective.

> *"While I keep my projects/tasks in Asana and some on my Outlook calendar, at the end of each day, I make a short list (on paper) of high-priority tasks that must be completed the next day so I know what I am walking into. That list serves as a place for me to note other things that come up the next day as well."*

My thoughts exactly, Laura. I've had clients say it seems inefficient to rewrite the list of priorities. But, as Anne pointed out from her Planner Pad, it is a funnel. The larger To-Do list keeps track of all of the projects, tasks, ideas, and to-dos. However, the daily priorities are often better memorialized and executed when they are written down again.

Decades of psychological research — from Daniel Kahneman and Amos Tversky's work on the *simulation heuristic* to Albert Bandura's studies on visualization — show that mentally rehearsing a scenario can improve planning, accuracy, and confidence. Through this *mental simulation* and real understanding of what you will need to do and how much time it will take to do it, it helps you remove friction from the next morning and reduce the stress of overcommitting. It's a practice of realistic scheduling that incorporates both fixed appointments and preparation or follow-up work around them. And it totally works. Let's practice one together.

Intentional Scheduling for Maximum Impact

You look at your calendar tomorrow, and on it you see:

- 10:30 a.m. Team Meeting
- 12:30 p.m. Client Lunch
- 5:30 p.m. Sports Activity

Upon initial glance, it doesn't seem like a busy day. Let's map out the journey of your day together with the Shut Down Routine.

You plan to start work at about 8:00 a.m., and you realize you will need about 15 minutes of planning for the Team Meeting and another 15 minutes for planning for the Client Lunch. You also need to leave at 5:00 p.m. to make it to your daughter's Sports Activity.

When reviewing the day through the lens of what it looks and feels like to live it, you also realize that the Team Meeting usually runs long, and, if we are being realistic and practical, we need to account for that extra time. You also figure that you need to start walking to the restaurant at 12:15 p.m. (instead of 12:30 p.m. as noted on our calendar).

When we add in that travel time and the longer meeting length, your day starts to look like this:

8:00 – 10:30	OPEN TIME
10:30 – 11:15	Team Meeting
11:15 – 12:15	OPEN TIME
12:15 – 2:00	Client Lunch (with commuting time included)
2:00 – 5:00	OPEN TIME

Now, let's merge Step Two and Step Three of the Shut Down Routine. We need to consider Preparation, Follow-Up, and what else we will do with that Open Time.

Our Open Time is 8:00 – 10:30 (2.5 hours), 11:15 – 12:15 (1 hour), and 2:00 – 5:00 (3 hours). Not too bad – a total of 6.5 hours of Open Time.

Until now, you often waste that valuable Open Time in the morning on remedial, low-risk and low-reward tasks and then throw up your hands later that this was just a Shit Day and the rest of the day is wasted.

Practicing the Shut Down Routine and mental simulation, and reviewing the Open Time, we ask ourselves if there is any Preparation or Follow-Up that we should consider. Then, we revise our Open Time like this:

8:00 – 10:30	OPEN TIME: • Prepare for Team Meeting (15 Minutes) • Prepare for Client Lunch (15 Minutes) • Finalize and send Proposal to Prospective Client (60 to 90 minutes) • Review emails (30 Minutes)
10:30 – 11:15	Team Meeting
11:15 – 12:15	OPEN TIME • Follow-up from Team Meeting (15 Minutes) • Review emails (15 Minutes) • Begin preparing Memo to Client (30 Minutes)
12:15 – 2:00	Client Lunch (with commuting time included)

2:00 – 5:00	OPEN TIME • Follow-up from Client Lunch (15- to 30 Minutes) • Review emails (30 Minutes) • Finalize and send Memo to Client (30 Minutes) • Focus on Big Project (60 to 90 Minutes)

While you do not necessarily need to note time estimates in your Shut Down Routine, I find it helpful to ensure you can realistically complete what you intend to do. Otherwise, since we tend to inflate how much we can accomplish in our open time, that morning Open Time Block will look like this:

8:00 – 10:30	OPEN TIME: • Finalize and send the proposal to the prospective client • Review emails • Write article • Reach out to 3 new prospects • Send Memo to Client • Start working on Big Project • Prepare for Team Meeting • Prepare for Client Lunch

Without the plan, you're hopeful to get probably two weeks' worth of things done in a two-and-a-half-hour block of time. It's wishful thinking.

Cal Newport, the author of *Digital Minimalism* and *Deep Work*, argues that this is a mistake many of us make. What we call our To-Do List is really our Wish List. You are doing this too. When you are not intentional, when you do not time-block and plan, you are essentially wishing you will get so much more done than is possible.

Those mistakes lead to beating yourself up for not getting as much done as you thought you would. You think your entire journey is derailed, when in reality, it is just a minor hijack on your path to the Perfectly Productive Day. And those detours are still a part of the journey. Let's check out some of the detours that might occur as you head towards your destination.

Detours Are Still Part of the Journey

You and I have now explored the Three-Step Process to the Perfectly Productive Workday and living an intentional workday. You need space on your calendar to get the Deep Work done. You need to identify what the top A1 project is to work on during the Deep Work block. And you have Internal and External barriers to grasp to get started and stay focused.

Of course, we are not robots who can do this every day, all day. Crap happens, stress increases, hijacks, and emergencies occur.

There are days when I have the best of intentions. I have space on my calendar, I know what I need to do, and I think that I've squashed all distractions. Then, something happens. Another Distraction Hijacks my Day – I call this an ADHD Moment. I use this acronym intentionally because I believe living with ADHD is common, and it is just a different way of thinking than a neurotypical brain. Whether someone has ADHD or not, we can all be easily distracted – and those distractions can take many forms. It could be that my son's bike was stolen…again. It could be that my husband called me to say he will be working late and can't grab the kids. It could be the doctor calling with my test results. It could be a client needing help with something right away. It could be my own thoughts, procrastination, or behaviors that were not supporting my desire to be intentional today.

All of these things occur. A Perfectly Productive Workday is knowing what it looks like and being able to reset when things go awry.

As I write this section in July 2025, I am coming off of a month that did not go as planned. To keep it brief, I had planned to be out of the office and mostly offline for two weeks at the beginning of the month. The week leading up to that trip was less productive than usual, as I used my Deep Work time to tie up loose ends before I was away. You've been here before, right?

Then, I was out of the office for two weeks. The little time I turned on my computer, it was primarily to work on the pages of this book because I wanted to. Everything else was on an extended pause.

When I returned to the office, I had two and a half days blocked to get caught up on emails, get organized, and get some of the Deep Work done that needed to be done. That time was used to catch up on emails, get the following week set up, and get some shallow projects done.

Ready to tackle the following week, nothing went as planned. Everything from a congested schedule to an influx of emails (people waiting until I was back, you know how that goes), to getting sick, and some other personal things that piled up; it felt like that week was super unproductive. I was getting frustrated and feeling behind. Each day, I would use my tools to reset again and then something else would go awry or get hijacked. You know what. It sucked. It really sucked.

But, instead of giving up and deciding that I just can't control anything, I aimed to reset daily and was successful in making progress each and every day as much as possible. A month that was not perfect was still a month full of progress and possibilities.

The takeaway is that we will all have setbacks, unproductive days or weeks, and bloopers in our workday. These detours on your journey to success are just that - detours - and shouldn't stop you from staying the course. If I were a betting woman, I'd guess that a detour on your road trip of a lifetime would not prevent you from redirecting back onto the main highway until you reached your destination. The daily detours of your workday are just a reminder that progress isn't always linear, but it's still progress when you choose to keep going.

Wrapping Up the Workday

Creating your Perfectly Productive Workday isn't about packing every minute or executing flawlessly. It's about aligning your time, space, and energy with your priorities—so you end the day with a sense of progress and success and not exhaustion and frustration.

You've learned how to design your day before it designs you, how to carve out meaningful time for deep, focused work, and how to identify and eliminate internal and external obstacles to your productivity. You've seen the power of boundaries, intentional routines, and the science behind your behaviors. Now, it's time to practice.

Start small. Protect one block of time. Run your first Shut Down Routine. Catch yourself when procrastination creeps in and ask, "What reward am I really chasing?"

Step by step, build habits that serve you and the Future You will thank you for it.

Remember, your Workday doesn't define your worth, but how you design it can elevate your impact, reduce your stress, and help you reconnect with what matters most.

You are not behind. You are just one intentional decision away from your next Perfectly Productive Day. Now, let's wrap up our Perfectly Productive Workday and get ready to transition to the personal responsibilities and commitments that are waiting for you on the other side of your commute home.

Evening Routine

"*The future depends on what you do today.*"

— MAHATMA GANDHI

CHAPTER 10

Shifting from Work Mode to Home Mode

One night, my oldest son and I went to dinner at The Yard House. My younger son and my husband were out of town. The children's menu had a fill-in-the-blank game to determine what the name of your rock band would be – sort of like a Mad Lib (remember those?). It was based on filling in a few nouns, a vegetable, a color, and an article of clothing.

This inspired my son and me to randomly name artists and songs. I would ask something like, "This band has a song called Bang, Bang, Bang."

"AJR," my son would exclaim.

Quickly running out of artists and songs to name, we turned it into Disney movies, and then it expanded to any movie. When my younger son and husband returned, we invited them to join us in this fun game we now call "Family Dinner."

The boys love Family Dinner and enjoy coming up with new clues for movies we've already guessed before. Ratatouille, for example, could have a clue about a rat who is a chef. It can also have a clue about a famous chef named Gusteau.

One of the things I love most about this activity is that it usually lasts ten to twenty minutes during dinner, where everyone is just…present.

The hours leading up to this moment of engaged conversation with the family are not so mindful. In fact, it is typically rush, rush, rush, crazy town, and an utter disaster of time. Yes, even productive people feel as though that period from after work to falling asleep is like entering a carnival fun house filled with smoke, mirrors, and hysteria. You're not alone.

It's Not You…Evenings are Crazy!

Evenings are madness. Right? After you've finished a long day of working, jumping in and out of meetings, you shut down your workday, only to open up a new can of worms. Or maybe it is a can of green beans to make with some chicken nuggets for the kids before you have to pile them up and head to soccer practice.

In the short hours of 5:00 to 9:00 p.m. (or you fill in what that block of time is for you), it seems you have to get as much done as you do in your entire workday. You have to drive them around town, sit in on their practice (or maybe get errands done at that time), feed the kids (maybe yourself), facilitate showers and toothbrushing, read stories, finish homework, feed the pets, and kiss those sweet little faces good night. Ok, ok, it is less of the "kiss the sweet little faces" and more like yell at them a million times to just go to bed!

By the time all of that happens, all you want to do is sit on the couch and scroll through social media on your phone. Or maybe you're itching to get back to work at this ungodly hour.

When you started this journey to create your Perfectly Productive Day, I told you that it is hard to start at any one point of the day because the Perfectly Productive Day is cyclical and contingent on your behavior at other times of the day. What you do now during your evening routine directly affects the Perfectly Productive Day you will have tomorrow. So, let's change your evening chaos now to become your Perfectly Productive Evening Routine.

Despite how tired you are. Despite how much work you need to do. Or how many high school friends you need to spy on, you will not do that tonight. No, tonight you will make a small behavioral change that will lead to healthier behavior and habits over time.

Separating Work from Personal

You are only one person. I know, groundbreaking. Stay with me. Because this is where things start to matter.

Think of it this way: you have one backpack, and everything you carry goes into it. Work projects, personal To-Dos, errands, deadlines, appointments, family needs. When everything is shoved into the same bag without any separation, the backpack becomes overstuffed, heavy, and frustrating to navigate. It's not that you're carrying the wrong things. It's that everything is mixed together, chaotic, and disorganized.

That's why it's important to separate work-related To-Dos and projects from personal ones. Clear boundaries – or bridges – help you know when you're on the clock and when you're not. Now, here's the caveat. Real life doesn't fit neatly into categories. Sometimes personal tasks have to happen during work hours, and sometimes work spills into the evening. That won't ever disappear completely. The goal is to make those moments the exception, not the rule.

Creating that separation starts with organizing and prioritizing your personal To-Dos. When you're clear about what needs to happen during the day, what can wait until the evening, and what belongs on the weekend, the backpack gets lighter. Not because you're doing less, but because everything is organized, intentional, and finally has its place.

Before we go any deeper into evening routines, I want to share a simple tool I use to stay on top of my personal tasks and create clear boundaries. Chances are, you've seen it before. They're usually stacked near the checkout during back-to-school season or sitting temptingly close while you're waiting in line for your favorite Starbucks drink at Barnes & Noble.

I'm talking about a day planner.

CHAPTER 11

Setting up Tomorrow Tonight

Every year in September, I run down to my local office supply store to pick out my day planner. The one that I typically select is not fancy. It doesn't have stickers or colorful flowers. While I love the look of those day planners, they are not practical for me. Don't be fooled by their charm. They will draw you in only to abandon you after the first date together.

If the colorful one brings you joy and meets your needs, then girl, you do you. If, however, you are feeling a little triggered right now because you've experienced abandonment after the first date with a planner in the past, then let me help you select the right one for you.

There are so many day planners on the market to choose from, and they all have different shapes, sizes, colors, feels, and content. The pages are filled with everything from a basic schedule to a page for designing and reflecting on your perfect day. So how do you pick one?

Buying a day planner with all the bells and whistles is like buying a bakery when you really just need a birthday cake. Depending on how you plan to use the day planner, there are really only a few basic needs to consider. Everything else is just icing on the cake…or potentially inedible decorations on the cake when they are just "extras" that you don't really need to use.

The day planner that I pick is an At-a-Glance 8" x 5" daily planner. I primarily use it to ensure the basic needs and habits of a planner are met. The Four Basic Needs and Habits of the Day Planner are:

1. Scheduling Appointments and Meetings
2. Future Plans
3. Daily Checking
4. Never Leave Tasks in the Past

Let's unpack those a little further.

1. **Scheduling Appointments and Meetings**. Day Planners are perfect for scheduling your time. It is necessary for a good planner to have a place to put scheduled appointments and meetings. One thing to be aware of is your personal preference for how much space you want to write in. Here are a few things to look out for:
   - Are you ok with hourly blocks?
   - Do you need quarter-hour blocks?
   - Are you fine with a weekly planner?
2. **Future Plans.** In many cases, a Day Planner is a great way to keep track of things you will need or want to do in the future. This is why I prefer a *daily day planner for my personal use (versus a weekly one*, for example).

My habit is to paper-clip things to specific days depending on the activity or triggering event. For example, a dentist appointment would go into my digital Outlook calendar, and I would paper-clip the card reminder to the scheduled day of my appointment in my day planner. When it comes to action items with an approximate date, I will paper-clip a reminder to the day I think the event will happen. I can also paper-clip bills to be paid on the date I mail the payment. (The paper-clip factory has me on their holiday card list, lol).

3. **Daily Checking**. Finally, the last habit when using a Day Planner of any type: You must check it every day. In fact, I recommend checking tomorrow before the end of today. Whatever is scheduled, paper-clipped, or assigned should conform to your understanding of what tomorrow looks like.

   If something cannot happen, that is where Habit #4 comes in.

4. **Never Leave Tasks in the Past.** Whatever Day Planner you use, I recommend clipping past days shut as a visual cue that that time is behind you. It is impossible to do any of the actions that were scheduled in the past. This means that anything undone—any meetings, tasks, or pieces of paper that trigger something you need to do —must be moved forward in time. By clipping your planner shut on past dates, you will reinforce this habit. The Future You will thank you for not leaving anything behind.

Planning Tomorrow with a Checklist

The Checklist Manifesto by Dr. Atul Gawande is one of the most impactful books that I have read. This book resonated with me because it validated some of the weird yet useful behaviors I have always done.

In the book, Dr. Atul Gawande explores how checklists can transform complex fields like medicine by standardizing essential steps. While visiting operating rooms, he observes high infection rates in catheter lines and discovers that simple, often overlooked steps contribute to the problem. By implementing a straightforward, step-by-step checklist for doctors and nurses to follow, he achieves a dramatic reduction in catheter-related infections. The checklist ensures that critical steps, such as hand-washing and proper sterilization, are consistently followed, highlighting the profound impact of simple tools in complex environments. This approach saves lives, reduces errors, and ultimately shows the power of a structured checklist in high-stakes situations.

Even the physicians in his study thought that the checklist was the dumbest idea ever. Yet its implementation was essential for saving lives. It worked in the operating room, and it works in my house every night.

Many years ago, I do not even recall when I first started doing this, I created this little notecard:

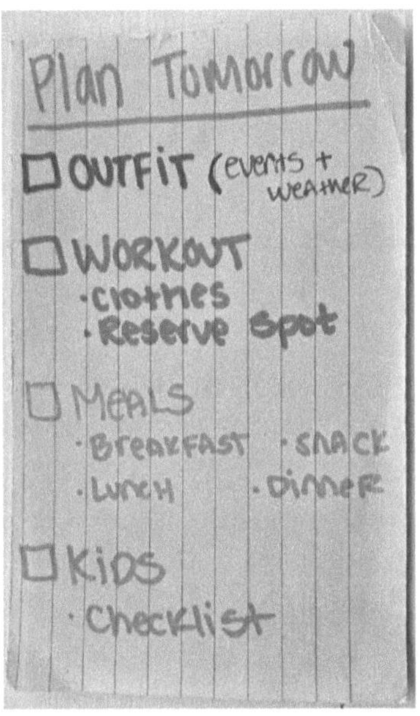

Every evening, I check the paperwork in my day planner, including this checklist, which I moved it to today after I completed it last night. When I see this little card, it is simply a checklist to remind me to prepare for tomorrow. Since we've already learned a lot about each other, I think I know what you're thinking:

What does this checklist mean to you, or what does it prompt you to do, Sarah?

I'm glad you asked.

This checklist invites me to pause and prepare for each category the next day. Running down the list, I assess my needs for tomorrow:

Clothes.

First, I decide what I am going to wear tomorrow. Usually, I take about 30 seconds to check two important considerations for my outfit tomorrow: the weather and my calendar.

If, for example, tomorrow is going to be hot and I have only virtual meetings, I will pick out a cute blouse and a pair of shorts or joggers. Business on the top and party on the bottom. If I have an in-person meeting, I need to decide what to wear instead of yoga pants.

Once I've decided what to wear, I pull it out and hang it on a hook in my bathroom.

Check.

Workout

Next, I will consider what my workout will be tomorrow. I mentioned in the Perfectly Productive Morning that I work out at OrangeTheory® Fitness. This prompt in my checklist reminds me to register for the class and to lay out my workout clothes on the bench in my bathroom.

Dan Beck is the same way, and being a former US Naval Officer, I am not surprised. Dan says,

> *"I schedule physical exercise, a fitness class I go to, in advance of the day. Sometimes in the morning, though most often in the afternoon or evening. I find that by scheduling it ahead of time on*

> *my calendar, it's more likely that I am going to commit to it and go, and not schedule over it."*

For many years, I would take the time during my evening routine to grab the workout pants, sports bra, workout top, socks, and sweat towel and make a pile. Then one day, it dawned on me while doing laundry: put these piles together into a stack when putting laundry away.

Now I have a shelf in my closet dedicated to these stacks, and I will put four to five of them together at a time. It's like my own workout outfit, Grab 'n Go. I'm always looking for simple ways to be more efficient and systematic. And if you're anything like me, you probably are too.

Back to the checklist: once I've registered for the class and laid out the workout pile on the bench in the bathroom, I am done preparing for my morning workout.

Check.

Meals

Next on the checklist is Meals. Under that, I break it down from Breakfast to Snack, Lunch, and Dinner. These prompts encourage me to pause and think, *"What am I eating tomorrow and when?"*

Feeding our bodies fuels our productivity. Now, this might be where you anticipate that I am going to tell you that I make smoothies every morning and eat salmon with roasted vegetables for lunch. Nope.

I suck at eating well. So much so that I see a health and wellness coach to help me try to eat better and improve my mindset around food and meals. I love the idea of being a healthy eater, but I just do not choose to spend most weekends planning, prepping, cooking, and dispersing meals. On some occasions,

I do, and I love the outcome and ease of having a healthy meal ready in the fridge, but these situations are the anomaly for me.

Instead, this checklist is to ensure I have a clear idea of what my meals will be for the next day. I also use a notepad in the kitchen to meal plan the same four meals throughout the day. Basically, the checklist is to review the meal plan and double-check that nothing has changed, or to pack any meals for lunch on the road, for example.

Check.

CHAPTER 12

Creating Stability at Home

Now onto the Kids section of the checklist.

Where do I start with this one?

In our home, we have a pretty clear division of labor in the mornings. My husband handles the kids' morning routine while I take the lead later in the day.

You see, he works evenings, so our responsibilities have naturally fallen into place. He is in charge of getting the kids up, fed, dressed, and out the door for school.

Magan Dobson, introduced earlier, has yet another parenting thing figured out. Her daughters pack their own lunches and snacks the night before, which is very smart. I would consider adopting that idea, except my evenings are already full, and my husband doesn't seem to mind the morning routine too much.

My role focuses on making sure afternoons and nights run smoothly, from pickups and homework to activities, dinner, bath time, and getting those sweet little heads onto their pillows at a reasonable hour.

My kids are a bit older at the time of writing this book, so the Kids Checklist has evolved over time.

When the kids were infants, the Checklist was a reminder of:

- Is the diaper bag packed and ready to go?
- Are there enough diapers, wipes, burp cloths, pacifiers, formula or breastmilk, and bottles for the day?
- Is there a clean change of clothes in there?
- What is the weather, and how should I dress them?

In the toddler ages, when they'd go to day care or grandmas for the day, the Checklist would ask:

- Do they have enough snacks?
- Do they need a clean change of clothes?
- Is their favorite blanket or teddy packed?
- Where is their activity bag?

Geo Derice, who served as the editor for this book, once shared a simple routine he uses to set himself up for smoother, more productive days. After helping his son with his evening bath, he leaves himself a visual cue for what comes next. In the bathroom, there is a bottle of body wash for bath time and a bottle of lotion for the following morning. After the bath, the body wash gets put away, and the lotion is left on the counter to greet Tomorrow Geo.

He has said that seeing the lotion in the morning signals that the day has already started with intention. Last-Night Geo made a small, thoughtful decision that helps Tomorrow Geo move forward with less friction. It reflects what researchers call the Progress Principle – and it's exactly why small decisions made the night before can change the entire trajectory of your next day.

You likely do something similar to get your kids ready each day.

Once the kids start elementary school, which is currently where my younger son is, then the Checklist changes to:

- Is their backpack packed and cleared out from the prior day?
- What are they eating for lunch, and is it made?
- What is their after-school activity or camp?
- Do they have their favorite blanket or teddy packed?
- What will the weather be like tomorrow, and what will they wear to school?

Now my sons are in the upper grades of elementary school, and the oldest is in middle school. Their Checklist has taken on a life of its own. My "Kids" Checklist is meant to direct my boys to their extensive Checklist.

Their lists are printed and put into a page protector, and they use a dry-erase marker to check off their tasks.

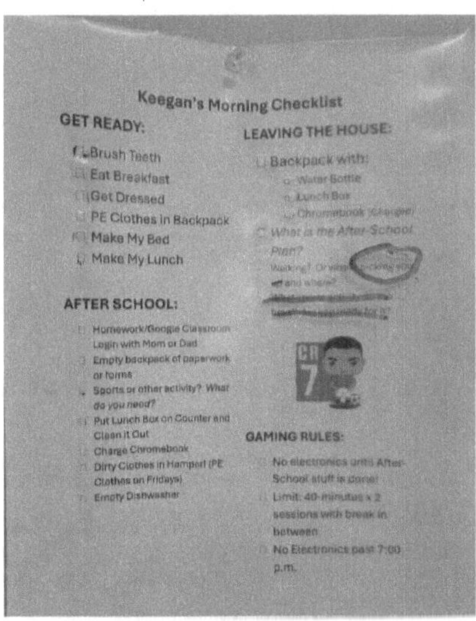

Having their own checklist helps my sons stay on track, manage their time, and gain responsibility.

My kids are not yet teenagers, but I imagine my Kids Checklist at that point will be:

- Give your kid a hug whenever you see him or her.
- Try to limit the length of time that they are on their phones.

We are frequently reminded that the days are long, and the years are short. This doesn't ring truer than the teenage years when you barely see them and when you do, they've locked themselves in their bedrooms.

You get the idea from the Kids' Checklist. That single word on my notecard, Kids, elicits curiosity for what is needed for the next day.

Check.

Having this daily checklist helps me run through those important things to plan ahead and set Tomorrow Me up for success. Once I complete those checklist items during my Perfectly Productive Evening Routine, I move the checklist notecard to the next day in my day planner.

Of course, knowing where to keep the day planner and where to find that checklist each night is also important. This is why you need a command center at home to track all of the important paperwork and To-Dos.

Command Center at Home

Almost every day, except Sundays and holidays, the mailperson delivers your mail to a physical mailbox. She or he drops the stack into your bin (or box or bucket) and walks away. Even if you are not someone who checks your mail daily, you are likely checking it regularly. What do you do with your mail at that point?

At the very least, it is recommended that you go through it when you pull it out of the mailbox. Throw away or recycle the easy decisions – the coupon books that you do not need or real estate listings that get a quick glance.

The rest of the mail, if it can't be fully processed that day, should live in a command center at your home. That could be a section of your desk. It could be a corner on the kitchen counter. It could be a dedicated table of its own. Whatever it is, it is where you will find unpaid bills, invitations sent by mail that have not been addressed yet (who sends invitations by mail anymore?), or coupons that you're interested in using.

My command center is a small table, similar to a night-stand, that sits in our living room. The drawer of the table contains my day planner, checkbooks, receipts folder, thank you cards, return address labels, extra pens, notepads, Post-it® notes, stapler, white-out, and similar office supplies. On top of the desk is a pen holder and a file sorter. The file sorter contains paperwork that still requires action.

In front of the file sorter are my current, unpaid bills, in order by due date. In the next section of the file sorter is information about a remodel we want to do someday. It is still an action item, which is why it is in this file sorter and not put away in my file cabinet, but it is not a high priority. I collect information about the remodel in that file folder. It's like my own printed version of Pinterest since I never caught on to that phenomenon. Behind that is miscellaneous information, such as my kids' school directory and our dream of buying a home in a village in Mexico. This drawer also holds my day planner, so I always know where to find it. Speaking of villages…

It Takes a Village

While we are certainly discussing the various ways that you can have a Perfectly Productive Day, it is also important to remember that sometimes we cannot do it all.

It does take a village.

Jennifer Stewart is the owner of Gateway Productivity in St. Louis, Missouri. She is a productivity tech guru, and I admire her and her work.

In a recent newsletter, Jennifer mentions a close friend who was recently diagnosed with a medical condition. Another friend responded with, "You are not alone."

As Jennifer says, those words are so simple, yet so powerful. She continues by letting her readers know to "*please remember that it is okay, even brave, to ask for help, no matter what you need. Do you need to lean on someone or request help with something that's causing you stress and anxiety?*"

What, if anything, can you delegate and take off your plate from your chaotic evening routine?

- Who can get your kid to practice so you can have some extra time to put the laundry away?
- Who can prepare dinner (hello Door Dash) so that you can help your daughter with her homework?
- Who can help you get the laundry put away before your kids are panicking and asking (AGAIN) where their baseball uniform is?
- What can wait until this weekend, when more hands are available, so that you can maximize your time and energy on this middle-of-the-week crazy night?

You are not alone.

It often feels that way. I get it. It happens to me too, especially since my husband works nights. I often feel alone and like I am doing a lot of it by myself.

That's why it is even more important to lean on your village whenever and wherever you are able to do so.

Pause right now and consider what you have going on this upcoming week. Who can you lean on to help you out? Stop letting all of those excuses take over your mind right now that are talking you out of asking that person. Pick up the phone and send that text or call that person.

> *"Hi, Mom? Are you able to help get Jaxon to swim practice on Thursday?"*

> *"Hey, Katie. Thanks for helping me out last week with the homework situation. Would you be able to help again tomorrow?"*

> *"Hi Husband (or Partner), will you please conceive, plan, and execute (CPE -- a framework from Eve Rodsky's Fair Play that assigns full ownership of a task from planning through completion) dinner on Friday night? I have a full day of meetings, and it'd be helpful not have to think about it at the end of the long week. Thanks!"*

Ask your kids for help unloading the dishwasher or with other chores they can assist with (assuming they are old enough). Even the smallest task, such as loading or unloading the dishwasher, can work wonders in ensuring the village runs efficiently and happily. And speaking of dishes....

Never Go to Bed Angry...at Yourself

Imagine this scene for a moment. You wake up and, after doing your morning stuff in the bathroom, you make your way into your kitchen to make coffee or tea. Upon arriving in that space, you are greeted with...

A counter full of dirty dishes.

How does that affect your mindset in the morning? Your initial reaction may be that it doesn't. However, it does affect your mood and productivity. The prior night, you might have been too exhausted to clean up the mess from dinner. So you left the pots and pans soaking near the sink – telling yourself that the "soaking" is effective. When the truth is, it is just the tiredness from last night that is delaying a task for the Future You to deal with.

Does this resonate with you?

Candidly, that was me almost every morning – up until writing this book. My husband and I used to have a terrible habit of leaving dirty dishes to handle the next day. As I write this book to help you and me both have a Perfectly Productive Day, I am more aware of this unproductive habit. The time invested in washing the dishes does not change whether we do it at night or in the morning. However, its impact on your mood, mindset, and productivity is significant.

According to the research, you should never go to bed angry...at yourself. One of the best things you can do in the evening is to wash the dishes. Research shows that cleaning up before bed — such as washing dirty dishes – can reduce stress, improve mood, and promote better sleep. Mindful dishwashing, in particular, has been linked to lower anxiety and greater inspiration, while a clean, uncluttered space helps lower cortisol levels and sets a calm tone for the morning. Even small nightly tidying habits can ease mental load and boost overall well-being.

While we are on the topic, let's discuss the most effective and productive way to load a dishwasher. Save time by loading the dishwasher: put spoons in the same slot, similar-sized plates next to each other, glassware with glassware, and mugs with mugs. Our human brains are designed to search for patterns. Loading the dishwasher with likes-with-likes satisfies our need to create patterns. Then, when you unload, your brain continues to find patterns in that and only needs to focus on a section rather than multitasking and having to think harder about what to put away.

Going to bed with the dishes done is still a work in progress for me, but one I do buy into, given this research and behavior, to ensure I start my day with a Perfectly Productive Morning.

Getting Cozy

Getting cozy for the night is one of my favorite things to do. There is something so satisfying about tearing off the clothes from the day, taking off the bra, and putting on my cozies. For some of you, this might fall into the Bedtime Routine section rather than the Evening Routine. My Perfectly Productive Evening Routine means I take off my work clothes and settle into my cozy pajamas sometime around dinner time.

This has also created a habit: I rarely leave the house after 6:00 p.m. unless we are still at a kids' sporting event. I'm not saying this is the best behavior, but it is my habit and enjoyable for me.

And since we are talking about our Perfectly Productive Day, let's also talk about laundry hacks that save us time. When removing your clothes, always take them off right-side out.

When doing laundry, do you often have to turn shirts, socks, pants, or other items right-side out again? Then you likely take your clothes off by flipping them inside out as you remove them. Save time by consciously removing your clothes right-side out. Your future laundry-doing-self will thank you!

A Place for Everything and Everything in Its Place

Mara Kent owns a travel agency (Adventures with Mara, LLC). She is a wife and mother of two children from Pleasant Hill, California. Mara says, *"I think my little efforts every day to do laundry and pick up around the house help me be more productive because I do a little bit of tidying up constantly throughout the day, and having a tidy home helps us think more clearly too."*

She isn't alone. Kiera Malowitz, CPO® and owner of Decluttered, LLC in Dallas Ft. Worth, Texas, has a similar reset habit.

> *"At the end of every day, I take twenty minutes to reset my house. I put anything left out in the main living areas back where it belongs, and I wipe down the kitchen counters. This way, I wake up each day feeling like I can start my day fresh with no visual clutter."*

Both of these women clearly value a clean, organized, and orderly home. In the evening, even when you're exhausted and all you want to do is watch Netflix or scroll social media, it's important to take a few minutes and put things back in their place.

There is a place for everything, and everything should be in its place. If you're doing this each time you use something – and asking your partner and children to do the same (with reminders, I know, I know – why can't they just get it the first time) – then this evening routine is not as time-consuming. Even if you think you'll use it again this afternoon, tomorrow, or next week, it is always more efficient to put things back in their homes. (Your wallet will also thank you since you won't spend money on things you already own.)

Recognizing this habit can be tedious and taxing, so I want to offer a few strategies. One of the secrets to doing this is to place things in the direction it needs to go. Suppose you need to put something away in your bedroom. If you aren't heading down the hallway (or up the stairs) at this very moment, place the object in a consistent place that will start to train your brain to act on autopilot so that anything set there means it needs to move in that direction.

Then, each time you walk that way, you pick up an item or two and put those things away. As with many things, completing tasks on a maintenance behavior (rather than waiting until they pile up) reduces wasted time and allows you to accomplish more.

If, while reading this, you're thinking to yourself, *"but I don't know where it belongs,"* or *"the drawer or cabinet that it belongs in is so full that I can't put it away."* This is a good time to consider working with a professional organizer to help purge and organize your stuff.

The professional organizing business has grown substantially in the past two decades, and you can find a professional organizer in just about any city in the United States and in and around major cities throughout the world. Google "professional organizer" or "home organizer," and you will find a plethora of qualified and amazing choices to work with.

There may be a number of reasons why you have not been comfortable working with a professional organizer, some of them might be:

- They cost too much.
- I'm afraid they'll start tossing everything I own.
- I'm embarrassed.
- I want to get organized before I bring them in.
- I'm so busy, I don't have time to manage that.

Let's briefly break down all of these excuses.

- **They cost too much.** It is true that professional organizers are often an investment. You can research and interview a few to find a good fit. Many offer packages of hours, which lowers the hourly rate.

  Most will also help you prioritize. Give them your budget and your goals. They can help determine what should be done first and within that budget, and even provide some insights and homework to work on other goals outside the budget.
- **I'm afraid they'll start tossing everything I own.** Consider working with an organizer who is a member of the National Association of Productivity and Organizing Professionals (NAPO®). NAPO® organizers are bound by a code of ethics. An empathetic, honest, and caring organizer would never throw away anything that you did not agree to.

  It is true that purging is often part of organizing; however, it will only happen when the organizer has buy-in from their client.
- **I'm embarrassed.** You might feel embarrassed, and the words on this page aren't going to change how you feel. And that's ok. Recognize the embarrassment for a moment and then turn that thought into a positive one. For example, when your mind draws up a story about the organizer judging you while going through

your bathroom drawers, remind yourself that this is what they do for a living. Just like your gynecologist sees thousands of vaginas, your professional organizer sees thousands of naughty and messy drawers.

- **I want to get organized before I bring them in.** Isn't it ironic and silly that we clean our house before the house cleaners get there? At least I do. Imagine going to the coffee shop and making your own coffee? Or ordering an Uber and asking the driver if you can operate the vehicle?

  Organizers are there to help you change your space and your habits. To be most effective, it is preferable to see the space in its native form. So, don't organize before the organizer arrives; they will handle it with you.

- **I'm so busy, I don't have time to manage that.** Many organizers prefer that the client work alongside them to help make the decisions. However, many organizers are okay with working alone. Organizers are organized, so they are used to separating objects in an orderly way.

  When I used to organize homes, I would make piles of likely donatable items, questionable items, and keep items. Then, I'd check with the client. Even short breaks in the day to check in will make a significant impact on your space.

  The energy it takes to make decisions while organizing is often draining. Therefore, I recommend that if you do need to schedule the professional organizer on a workday, then you do so for a day that affords you the opportunity to work on lower priority tasks and not a meeting-heavy day where you'll be more exhausted.

Now that you've been educated and your fears have been squashed, consider taking the first step of researching or calling an organizer in your area. I finally did.

Recently, I hired a professional organizer myself. While I am capable of organizing my kitchen and knew exactly what I needed and wanted to do, the task at hand seemed daunting to handle alone, and I wasn't successful in getting my husband to eagerly raise his hand on a Saturday.

I reached out to a former colleague, Karen Schroter of Orderly Outcome in Walnut Creek, California, and we tackled the project together. It took us six and a half hours to fully organize my kitchen. And I was so happy with the results. The family has even been more successful at keeping it clean and organized.

Admittedly, there were times when I was a little embarrassed by a greasy pan left at the back of the cabinet. Or I would be curious if Karen was judging our snack choices. I would actively set aside my negative self-talk and remind myself that, just like your gynecologist, Karen has seen it all, and part of her important role is to come in without judgment or criticism.

Consider hiring help; I promise that you will be so glad that you did. Clearing the clutter and organizing your external environment is a step in the right direction of controlling your mind and internal environment, which, as we know, can certainly get out of control during the chaos of the evening, and sometimes it feels like the only way to manage is to disconnect. Let's explore what you might want to do instead of disconnecting by doomscrolling or binge-watching.

CHAPTER 13

Protecting Your Evening Energy

The evenings tend to be a trigger time for many of us. There are many reasons this may be true. The first is that we truly are exhausted by the time the evening rolls around. And when we are exhausted, our serotonin levels are low, and we crave mindless activities and doing the easiest thing possible.

But it's time to change. It is time to develop healthier habits and behaviors to create a Perfectly Productive Evening Routine. Once they become a habit, they do not require much energy to maintain.

Evenings, in some situations, may also be triggering because they bring back memories of childhood and it being a challenging time in the household. Our parents were exhausted in the evenings, just like us, but they were less interested in self-awareness to change. Their behavior in the evening might have been slightly unhinged, a bit erratic, and utterly stressed out. The little you saw and personalized some of the behaviors of your parents – yelling, overwhelm, drinking, or silent treatments. Of course, this is not true for everyone, but is true for many of us.

Avoiding Excessive Drinking

Starting in late 2020, I began having a glass of wine or two in the evenings at home. Sometimes my children and I would go hang out at a friend's house (our kids went to the same distant learning school, so we were already very much exposed to each other). We would open up a bottle of Rosé. Then maybe two bottles. This became my new evening routine. Forget about *Rosé All Day*, it was *Rosé all Evening*.

My kids and I were still on a strict bedtime schedule, so we would depart by about 7:30 p.m. Arriving home shortly after, I would coordinate the kids' bedtime routine and then usually crawl in bed myself, falling asleep quickly because I was exhausted and the alcohol made it easy to do so.

The alcohol would numb my emotions, my stress, my frustrations, and my tiredness from working all day and helping with schoolwork in the afternoons. It also ensured that I was not set up for a Perfectly Productive Evening, a Perfectly Productive Sleep, nor a Perfectly Productive Morning. It only falsified my feelings at that moment.

Recognizing that my behavior was not who I was, I decided it was time to take charge. And so, I changed.

While still enjoying alcohol in some situations, I made a lifestyle change, electing to consume wine and alcohol much less frequently.

Even since starting the journey of writing this book, I prioritized early mornings on the weekends to get the words written on the page. This new lifestyle meant I would wake up early on Saturday and/or Sunday, get dressed, grab my laptop, and head to a coffee shop to write. This book was my priority, and writing in the mornings on the weekend was the schedule that worked best for me.

It didn't come easily to decline Friday night drinks and games because of the goal of getting up the next day to write. But, as we learned about procrastination and thinking about the Future You, I would remind myself of who I wanted to be on Saturday morning and make a smarter decision on Friday night.

Even while writing this book, there would be an occasional evening that my family and I would hang out with friends, and I'd forget my priorities. And if I am honest (which I am), sometimes it was the alcohol – tasting so good, the feeling so liberating – and the social situation addicting, I'd drink one or two too many. And of course, that means the next morning, I would not write. I would forgive myself, we all make mistakes, but I would remind myself that being the Perfectly Productive Me is my goal, and that includes honoring my commitment to work on my book on Saturday mornings so that I could get it published by my goal date of early 2026.

So, here we are – enjoying and learning from this book together. Which also means I have to remind myself to at times resist the urge to choose the more pleasurable thing in the moment, to end the socializing, put down my book, or pause my show in order to respect the Tomorrow Me decision.

Trading Cliffhangers for Calm

I used to work for a family-owned business, and often I would work out of the back, vacant office to focus on some projects. The owner, Jack, had bought a TiVo and the box sat in that office with me. I remember looking at the box and thinking how cool it was that an invention came out that could pause live television. To think of all the reality trash shows I missed because of studying, being out with friends, or sleeping.

Now, the kids have it so easy. Most of us rarely watch cable television anymore, instead subscribing to a streaming platform that, on the one hand, gives us back so much time in not having to watch commercials, and on the other hand, only heightens our inability to ever be bored.

Netflix or Hulu, or Amazon Prime, or Peacock, or YouTube, or, or, or ... you fill in the blank. There are so many streaming channels that I have lost count. You probably have also lost count. It seems as though every time I am told I must watch a new series, I am signing up for a free month with a new or reengaging streaming channel.

It's exhausting.

You're addicted to the streaming services and, like many habits that we've already established, it is not your fault. The researchers behind the series you watch have literally invested billions of dollars to keep you addicted to their shows.

In the evening, you are sucked into watching your favorite docuseries, dramas, and other shows on streaming services designed to make it impossible to stop at the end of an episode. Often, the best of intentions to just watch the rest of this episode and then go to bed get thrown out the window when the ending entices you to hit play on the next episode to find out what is going to happen next.

Mihaly Csikszentmihalyi , in the book *Flow, The Psychology of Optimal Experience*, says,

> *"The flow experience that results from the use of skills leads to growth; passive entertainment leads nowhere."*

He continues with *"Most jobs and many leisure activities — especially those involving the passive consumption of mass media — are not designed to make us happy and strong. Their purpose is to make money for someone else."*

You have to develop the habit or the willpower to know when enough is enough for the evening, and there are a few techniques that we will discuss.

One technique is to have a bedtime, which we will cover more thoroughly in the next section. The other technique is to clearly define how much you will watch. Defining how much you are going to watch could be done by defining the length of the show or by defining the stop point in time. Let me explain.

Defining the Length of the Show. Suppose you are currently watching a series with 45-minute episodes. You might set a pace of watching one or two episodes each evening. And that's it.

You can expect that, at the end of that defined period, you will want to watch more. I know, I know…it is so hard. You must find out what is going to happen to their marriage ***right now***!! But that's exactly how you get sucked into watching it for too long and not actually going to bed. You are in control here, not the show. You said you were going to watch one episode for 45 minutes, then transition to the bedtime routine or go to bed.

Defining the Stop Point by Time. The alternative approach is to set a timer on your phone for the length of time you will watch it. Say you start watching at 8:00 p.m. and want to start your bedtime routine at 9:00 p.m. Obviously, your goal is to watch for an hour. But, as you've frequently experienced, that often turns into 9:10 p.m., 9:20 p.m., or even 11:00 p.m. before you know it.

Instead, set a timer for that hour. I know it seems ridiculous that we have to set a timer to stop watching television. Inside our functional adult brains is a tiny person who developed and flourished with boundaries, rules, and external support. As adults, we have flipped that script and think we can just do it all on our own, or we must be failures. The internet is flooded with memes that mock our childlike mindset and behavior. But often the funniest jokes are the ones that we can relate to. As a mature woman in your forties, you still need help setting boundaries and rules, and with external support. A timer provides that.

Now, when that hour is up, when it is 9:00 p.m., and you need to stop watching television so you can invest time and energy in your Bedtime Routine, I promise you that you will want to keep watching. Especially the first time you try this method. What works for me is to allow myself to finish the current scene. At the hour mark, it is unlikely that you will be at the perfect transition point in your show. Allow yourself the extra thirty seconds to three or four minutes to finish that scene.

Not everyone has the discipline to STOP reading, or watching Netflix, or playing games. One of my colleagues is an incredible attorney specializing in helping franchise businesses grow and succeed. Dawn Newton and I were in a troika (this is a fancy word for a three-person networking meeting), and I mentioned this habit to Dawn. She said,

> *"I could never read at night. Once I start, I can't stop, and I will read into the wee hours of the morning. It is great if you can develop the habit of stealing the benefits of tomorrow from your tomorrow-self."*

I love how she said this, by the way — stealing the benefits of tomorrow from your Tomorrow Self.

You might be like Dawn. If you are cringing at my suggestion to hit stop in the middle of an episode, I have a different solution for you. Instead, here is your approach. When you sit down at 8:00 p.m. to start the episode that you are on, you check how long that episode is. If it is about an hour or less, you're good. You can watch that entire episode, then turn off the television. If, however, the episode is an hour and twenty minutes. You have to decide how you want to handle that. Are you now staying up an additional twenty minutes? Is there another show you can start instead?

Even though yesterday you couldn't pause in the middle of an episode, maybe this new you, this even more Perfectly Productive version of you, is okay with giving that a try, and you will get 80% of the way through the episode tonight. Knowing how much time you have and how long the episode is gives you the information you need to decide. And we know that knowledge is power.

Apps, Addictions, and Alternatives

Speaking of knowledge being power, we lie to ourselves that we are on social media to gain social knowledge about our society, our friends, our family, and our community. What we are really gaining is drama and emotional numbness.

The doomscrolling we do in the evenings or during quick breaks at work numbs the pain of exhaustion, stress, and other emotions. It does little else.

It isn't very often that you visit Facebook or Instagram and think to yourself, "*That was a productive use of time,*" or "*I really learned a lot from that social media visit.*" Right?

Usually, a visit to those sites results in heightened negative emotions, unnecessary purchases, frustrated reactions to other people's comments or posts, and wasted moments in your life.

In fact, according to Dr. Adam Alter, a Professor of Marketing at New York University's Stern School of Business, research has shown that the average person will lose twenty years of their life on "Doom Scrolling."

Twenty years.

Twenty years.

I am repeating myself because I really want you and me both to understand this.

You do not have to be included in this statistic. I do not want to be either.

How can we change our behavior to limit how much time we doomscroll?

Each year, I set a reading goal, like twenty-three books in 2023. That simple target helps me reach for a book instead of doomscrolling when I am bored, stressed, or running low on energy. It turns those small in-between moments, even waiting rooms, into chances to do something meaningful rather than mindless. Speaking of reading, if you'd like to join a book, we have an unofficial book club that can be found by visiting www.perfectlyproductiveday.com/resources.

In our Perfectly Productive Morning Routine, we spoke about my habit of reading in the lobby of OrangeTheory® Fitness. Most people I see are on their phones, likely doomscrolling to pass the time. But not you or me. We are doing something we enjoy ,and that helps us show up as our most productive selves.

I love getting lost in fictional books. I enjoy constantly learning and absorbing information in self-help and business-related genres. I geek out on productivity books.

An amazing productivity book that I have read is Cal Newport's *Digital Minimalism.* In the book, Cal argues that technology should serve as a tool to support your values, not dominate your life. By intentionally limiting digital distractions and focusing only on tools that provide real value, you can reclaim time, attention, and deeper human connections.

While reading the book, Cal challenged me to analyze and remove any apps on my phone that were not necessary. At the onset of this assignment, while certainly not perfect at mitigating distractions, I thought I was fully aware of unnecessary tapping on my smartphone.

Initially, I thought to myself that I really only use five apps on my phone: Outlook, Yahoo, my text messaging app, Duolingo, and Facebook.

Easy peasy.

I will get rid of Facebook for the month and reduce my usage of the rest to necessary check-ins only.

Boy, was I wrong.

I started writing down every time I opened an app. There was a list of about twenty-five apps that I visited often. Not five, but twenty-five.

Then I assessed whether it was *Required* or if that app was better defined as a *Distraction*.

Cell Phone (Apps):

D) • DUBSADO   X   Use for 1 learning session per day and <15 minutes.

D) • Outlook   X   Remove
        ↳ On Computer only

D) • Yahoo!   Only check up to 3x/day and <10 minutes each time.

D) • ~~Facebook~~   X   (don't need?) Remove

D) • Amazon   OK for necessary shopping only

R) • ~~FB Messenger~~   X   (don't need)

D) • Text Messages   Need to use/keep

R) • Good Reads   only to update books - 3-4x/month

D) • Castbox Podcasts   OK to use when appropriate.

D) • Chrome   LIMIT/BE AWARE.

R) • You Tube   X   DISABLED
R) • ~~Next Door~~   CAMERA removed
R) • Google Maps   X   avoid using
R) • Venmo   Only as needed
D) • Orange Theory   ok to use to check into
                                  classes daily
D) • Camera Gallery   ok for internal use
D) • Authenticators / LP   ok as needed
R) • ~~BART/Muni Transportation~~ X   Removed
R) • Banking (Chase, Citi, C1)   X   Be mindful of use
R) • McDonalds   X
R) • Cash App   ok for limited purpose
R) • Lyft/Uber   ok if needed in this area
R) • ~~IG~~   X   Removed
D) • Netflix, Hulu, etc.   ok for shows - limit
                                  @ lunch + before bed
R) • MS Planner   ok for quick updates

As a result of this exercise, I removed about a dozen apps from my phone and have not missed any of them.

The most rewarding thing was removing Facebook and Instagram. If I need or want to check what is happening socially, then I do so on my computer. Like many habits, I suspect I should revisit this exercise annually. Somehow, those pesky little apps make their way back onto the phone without you realizing it.

I want to check in with you. What do you think? Are you ready to review the apps on your phone and remove any that are not required? Or maybe you want to set a goal, reading more is an example, that will support you in investing in that activity at moments when you otherwise might choose to doom scroll.

Whatever you decide, try it out. I suspect you will fall in love with the Perfectly Productive version of you.

Setting Up Your Perfectly Productive Phone

It's your turn now. I'd recommend you pull out your phone right now to do the Perfectly Productive Phone exercise in the Perfectly Productive Day Workbook. While it may feel boring or painful or torturous, I promise you this entire exercise can be done in less than thirty minutes. If you don't have thirty minutes right now, then put a bookmark here and come back a little later today. Maybe after you finish watching your favorite episode a little earlier tonight.

When you do the exercise, I suspect you will find a few buckets that the apps fit into:

- Default Apps
- Forgotten Apps

- Required Apps
- Distraction Apps

The first two, Default and Forgotten Apps, will be easier to decide on. However, the Required Apps and the Distraction Apps will require a little more thought, and this is where it will get more difficult and tricky. These apps were downloaded to your phone at some point, and you most likely use them.

In *Digital Minimalism*, Cal encourages you to really assess whether they are Required or a Distraction. Some will be obvious, but most of them, your instinct will be to say to yourself, "*Oh, this app is* **Required**."

The question is, *are you being honest with yourself?*

You would likely argue that an app like Maps is 100% required. What Cal encourages you to consider is whether that is in fact true or if you are just so accustomed to it that you believe it is required.

Now, Maps may not be the best example because I understand your argument that it is **Required**. But let me just demonstrate what your line of thinking would be on this.

If the Map app did not exist, would you survive? Yes.

Is it necessary or a nice-to-have? Well, a little of both.

What would you need to do to succeed without that app? Well, when I was in college, apps did not exist. I would look up the directions on MapQuest and print them out. Or, even earlier in my life, MapQuest didn't exist, and I'd have a Thompson guide in my car.

Now, it is 2025 and we have the convenience and luxury of having a Maps app on our phones. And I would probably note this App as Required because I am not going to go through the trouble of reactivating my MapQuest login (if one still even exists and it wasn't bought out by Google Maps).

But when you are completing this exercise for the Required and Distractions Apps, I want you to really consider whether that app is *needed* or simply a *convenience* for you. Perhaps that Dutch Bros. coffee app could be removed.

The first time that I completed this exercise, I had an app on my phone that I identified as Required. It was an app that was needed to ride BART, our commuter transportation system here in the Bay Area.

When I rode BART daily, I used that app daily. Here's the deal now: I do not ride BART on a regular basis anymore. Maybe once per month. So, while I noted it as Required, I decided to remove myself from that clutter, and I deleted it. Nowadays, it is so easy to reinstall an App in seconds when needed. The ROI (return on investment) of deleting that Required App, knowing I would just download it again when needed, was liberating.

After completing the Perfectly Productive Phone exercise, I promise you will see an immediate ROI. You will feel lighter, freer, and in control.

I have found that being present and mindful has been a beautiful gift. Recently, my kids and I were standing in a long line, and I looked around. Most of the people in line around us were helping to pass the time by scrolling on their little devices. I've been there too. I've been the one standing there on my phone looking at who knows what.

In that moment, standing in line and engaging in conversation with my kids, it felt incredible. It felt like the real me.

"Underscoring the sheer quantity of the time that can be reclaimed when you sidestep mindless digital activity to once again prioritize the real you."

I'm so excited to be on this journey with you to prioritize the real you. Are you starting to find it in yourself? Because I see who the real you is, and she is awesome and truly a remarkable person.

Closing the Day with Intention

Your Evening Routine is more than just winding down from the day's chaos. It's the bridge between who you were today and who you want to be tomorrow. Each small action, from washing the dishes to laying out tomorrow's clothes, sends a signal to the Tomorrow You that you are cared for and supported. These rituals are not about perfection; they're about creating a calm, intentional close to one chapter so the next can begin with clarity.

By prioritizing preparation, tidiness, and boundaries, you set the stage for a more focused and productive tomorrow. And when life feels overwhelming, remember that you don't have to do it all on your own – lean on your village, delegate where you can, and let go of the myth that productivity means doing everything yourself.

As Gandhi wisely said, *"The future depends on what you do today."* Tonight's choices — however small — are tomorrow's momentum. A Perfectly Productive Day doesn't start with your morning alarm; it begins the night before, in those quiet, intentional moments when you decide to prepare, reset, and give yourself the gift of a fresh start. Now, let's explore setting yourself up for a restful night.

Bedtime Routine

. . . .

CHAPTER 14

Establishing a Bedtime That Works

"3 0 minutes until bedtime!"

"10 more minutes!!!!"

"It's bedtime!" we shout at our children every night. Yet, this is suddenly the time that they need to brush their teeth, watch five more minutes of their show, drink water, or pet the cats. You're tracking, right?

The bedtime routine for our kids is often wilder than a dog chasing a squirrel at a dog park. There is a reason there is a book called, Go the F--k to Sleep. If you haven't heard the story narrated by Samuel L. Jackson, I highly recommend you bookmark this page and look it up. It is worth the temporary distraction that is normally discouraged.

Now that you've been highly entertained by The King of Cool, I'll do my best to keep you entertained...and productive.

Let's set the scene of where you are in your day since you got a little distracted with the Go the F--k to Sleep narration and the digital distraction exercise.

You have now had a long, worthwhile, and productive day. You've started off with your Perfectly Productive Morning. You maximized your time on your Perfectly Productive Commute and batched tasks. Your Perfectly Productive Workday kicked ass. You didn't get everything done, but you got the right things done. After work, you had a Perfectly Productive Evening Routine, equipped with after-school activities, processing your incoming mail, fueling your body, and maybe indulging in some guilty pleasures. Now, it is time for bed.

The Power of a Bedtime

I have an important question to ask you. Do you have a Bedtime Routine? Do you even have a bedtime? No, really, if your immediate response to those questions is that they sound ridiculous and that you do not need a bedtime, well, I think you know in your heart that you do. Adults are really just high-functioning toddlers. Research consistently has demonstrated that human beings benefit from having a bedtime and a consistent Bedtime Routine.

Katie Burke is an awesome attorney in San Francisco focusing on navigating turmoiled relationships via family law and workplace investigations. You met her during our Perfectly Productive Commute this morning. When I posed the million-dollar question on LinkedIn – *What do you do to ensure you have a Perfectly Productive Day?* – Katie answered,

Katie Burke · 1st   1y •••
Family Law

I wish the yesterday me had been mindful of this when she finished binge-watching Breath of Fire (a yoga cult documentary), then proceeded to watch the entire Martha Stewart documentary—both very good, but neither disappearing off the platform any time soon (or probably ever).

Mine is honoring my nightly iPhone sleep reminder, which chimes at 8:00 p.m. to let me know I have an hour left before it's time to go to sleep. Since I set it years ago, I've ignored it every single night. Such a bad habit and so reversible. It's difficult for me because I go out almost every night (not partying—it's dinners and plays and other cultural events), but I'm almost always home by 9:00 p.m.

Recognizing that Katie is getting in her own way, she continued by saying,

So the discipline step for me is to start associating my arrival home with sleep, not TV time. On the rare nights when I go straight home after work, I can learn all about Martha Stewart's life if I want to (and I recommend everyone does; she's fascinating!). But if I'm going to keep up with my active lifestyle—which I am—then binge-watching when I get home has to go.

I can't say I'll go from denying future me this gift to a perfect record, but this is a huge 2025 goal for me. Thank you for the reminder, Sarah!

I would just add, Katie, that you should start your Bedtime Routine instead of binge-watching when you get home.

Additionally, having a bedtime starts to train your mind and body when it is time to go to sleep, which also keeps your circadian rhythm regulated. Having your internal clock programmed has many physical, social, and biological benefits. So, let's get your bedtime set so that your internal clock is functioning well again.

I am going to challenge you to set an alarm on your phone for the time that you should go to bed, but not yet. Don't do it just yet though, because 1) you are not bought into the value of having a Bedtime Routine, and 2) you do not yet know what time to set that alarm for. In fact, you might be thinking the wrong time altogether. So, let's establish some trust and a foundation on the topic, and then we will set that alarm.

Breaking the Bedtime Rebellion

When I lived in Santa Barbara, I used to go to a kickboxing class at Gold's Gym with an incredible instructor named Jenny. Jenny had crazy energy, was loud (but not in an obnoxious way), and she was extremely motivating.

Jenny soon opened her own boot camp, and some of my friends and I were addicted. Jenny Schatzle has grown her brand and is now a motivational speaker, fitness guru, mini-celebrity, and a wife and mom. And she's real – like really real.

Recently, on her feed, she posted about bedtime revenge (we'll talk about that a little later). She posted:

Dear moms,

Please take 30-60minutes of downtime
today.

Nap. Watch a show. Eat a full meal by
yourself and really enjoy the food. Sit on a
bench, at the beach, on your couch. Read
a book or magazine. I don't care if it's
10am. 4pm. After dinner at 6:30 while you
let your kids watch a show. Make some
time for yourself today.

*And Don't wait until the end of the night
and complete numb out by Bingeing TV,
doom scrolling, wine or food binge that
leaves you feeling like sh*t in the morning.
Take better care of yourself during the day
and you won't need to numb out at night
🤍.

Sincerely,
A mom who's managed her nighttime
numb out.

We explored doomscrolling and binge-watching during our Evening Routine, and at that time we put a pin in discussing the bedtime revenge. You know what it is because you might be doing it, but you may not have ever given it a name.

Like you, we were both familiar with procrastination for doing something that you need to do – Working on that research. Writing that memo. Sending that email.

We had also heard of procrastinating on some personal activities, such as going to the gym. Or even waking up in the morning.

But I had never heard of sleep procrastination until I was writing this book, and now it is coming up everywhere.

Let me clarify, I had heard of the behavior of not going to bed when you should, but I never knew it had an official psychological definition. And there is some serious research around sleep procrastination.

Sleep procrastination, also known as Revenge Bedtime Procrastination, is the act of intentionally putting off sleep and avoiding going to bed to do something else. It is an epidemic that can negatively affect sleep quality and lead to poor self-regulation.

Does this sound like you? Are you someone who rebels against bedtime and procrastinates falling asleep?

Some of the thoughts going through your head when you have revenge bedtime procrastination might be:

- *"I just want time for myself."*
- *"I want to watch this show or read this chapter."*
- *"It's the only quiet time I get all day."*
- *"I'll just scroll for a few minutes to unwind."*
- *"I deserve this time after everything I did today."*
- *"I'm just going to do a little bit more of work."*

"Instead of worrying about how we can more efficiently induce sleep, we need to stop resisting it."

According to the sleep experts, revenge bedtime procrastination is caused by stress and overwhelm. Often, it is because you put in long hours at work and now you want more time for yourself. Or you're just exhausted from the day and all of the decisions you had to make throughout the day. Or, after the kids *finally* go to sleep, you deserve some quiet time.

Sleep procrastination could also be caused by trauma, anxiety, depression, or ADHD tendencies. Some people report revenge bedtime procrastination due to peer pressure to keep hanging out or playing an interactive online game together longer.

Ultimately, it is also the result of not having healthy habits and systems in place to know when to go to bed and why. When faced with the crossroads of enjoying one more brainless reality TV drama episode versus deciding to fight falling asleep, the reality TV show wins because it feels like the easier decision in that moment.

But as Katie pointed out, the discipline to stop the fun, exciting activity and instead do the hard work of trying to fall asleep is critical to your overall health and productivity.

While writing this book, my Saturday routine was to wake up and go to OrangeTheory® Fitness and then go next door and write at a coffee shop (or sometimes vice versa). My friend, Jacqui, works at the front desk at OrangeTheory® and often pops into the coffee shop while I am still sitting there working.

One morning, we were speaking about this book and its theme. We discussed The Perfectly Productive Bedtime Routine and Sleep. Jacqui admitted that she often scrolls Instagram for up to an hour, sometimes before going to bed. Some of my clients have reported similar behavior at bedtime – whether it is shopping, working, doom scrolling, or watching something.

Jacqui walked into the coffee shop one Saturday morning and was thrilled to report she was investing in a new routine. Motivated by the theme of The Perfectly Productive Day and a desire to accomplish her goals, Jacqui excitedly told me that she had started putting the phone down earlier and meditating to help her fall asleep. This small shift in her routine made significant differences in her sleep, her mindset, and her behavior.

If you are someone who is currently doing something to protest bedtime, consider whether that activity is serving you. If not, like many things we have established and discussed throughout this book, it is not your fault. You are just another victim of our environment. We now live in a world where the attention marketplace has taken over our minds, bodies, and behaviors. It is actually *harder* now to do the thing that our mind and body *need and craves* than it is to do the thing that is easy, thoughtless, and exciting.

As a side note, the area of my life where I really struggle with this concept is food. If you think about it, our mind and body craves and needs natural foods – meats, vegetables, fruits, seeds, and nuts. And yet, we often ignore what we know to be true in favor of what we know to be easy. When I am stressed, tired, and hungry, I will drive through a McDonald's drive-thru before putting together the salad and grilling the chicken in my fridge. I am working on changing my Perfectly Productive Diet, but this book is not about that.

When you choose to watch another show, or even reading another chapter over falling asleep, you are really choosing the McDonalds easy way out over the farm-to-table cuisine your mind and body need.

So, how do you change? Well, you use tools, systems, and habits to make bedtime a defined part of your day. You eliminate the decision about your bedtime tonight, and instead, your bedtime is defined and acted upon based on a mathematical formula. Yes, I just used bedtime and mathematical formula in the same sentence. If nothing else puts you to sleep, maybe this chapter will. It sounds complicated or difficult; it isn't. We will figure out your unique mathematical formula shortly, and once we do, you will find that deciding when to go to bed is one less decision you will need to make.

CHAPTER 15

Understanding Your Sleep Needs

Most of the 35,000 decisions we make each day are made by our subconscious because we have developed systems and habits to make those decisions easy with filters, instead of making a conscious and active decision.

Think about it. Which hand should I grab the toothbrush with? My right hand. That's a decision that was made by habit and therefore not an active decision.

Do you want lettuce, tomatoes, and onions on your hamburger? Um, onions and tomatoes only, please. That's a slightly more active decision, but one that is mostly an autopilot decision.

What should I work on now? Finalizing the client memo? Drafting the proposal? Writing that article? Responding to that RFP? These decisions are intentional and active decisions, the ones that drain you faster (which is why we worked on those during our Perfectly Productive Workday).

The fact that we make over 35,000 decisions each day is as exhausting as it sounds. That is why it is important to mitigate the decisions you need to make whenever and wherever you can.

Dr. Lisa MacLean is the Director of Physician Wellness of the Henry Ford Clinic in Michigan. She is also an expert on decision fatigue, which says that the more decisions you have to make throughout the day, the more fatigue you develop. It is cumulative and gets worse throughout the day.

This is not unfamiliar to you. Often, after you've completed your morning routine, you are energized, productive, and feel great. By the time you finish work and you are transitioning into the evening, you are so decision-fatigued that all you want to do is doom scroll all night.

That decision to doom scroll – yes, it is still a decision and a habit – is unhealthy and leading to the cyclical behavior. Let's change that now.

Establishing a Bedtime Routine and a consistent bedtime pays dividends to your Perfectly Productive Day. Let's establish what that looks like for the Perfectly Productive You!

First, let's determine what time you should fall asleep. This is done by answering two important questions:

- How many hours of sleep do you need?
- What time do you need or want to wake up tomorrow?

Your answer might be *I don't know* to one or both of those questions. That's ok because we are going to answer that question together now, which might even mean modifying your immediate response to those questions to be something different than what you initially thought. Let's dive in together.

How many hours of sleep do you need?

Were you able to answer that question, or was your initial response *I don't know*? If you were quick to answer anything for less than eight hours, you likely are lying to yourself.

Wait, stay with me. I know I just lost some of you who are thinking, "*You don't know me, Sarah. I do NOT need eight hours of sleep.*"

You may be right. Not all of you need eight hours of sleep, and not all of you are lying to yourself. But let's explore this a little further.

For those who answered less than eight hours of sleep, it is more likely that you typically only **get** that amount of time, and you have now assumed it is all that you need. That used to be me. Then, the Perfectly Productive Me realized that I actually need eight to nine hours of sleep more often than not.

In order to determine your bedtime mathematical formula, or how many hours of sleep you truly need, for one week, try to fall asleep without setting an alarm. Document the approximate time you fell asleep and the time you woke up naturally – without snoozing. Better yet, use a tracker, such as a smartwatch. Do this for a week and see how long you are sleeping on average. It is probably longer than the length you initially answered. Now, obviously, you want to try and do this without sleeping inhibitors or getting up for hours in the middle of the night. More on that in the Perfectly Productive Sleep section. The point of this exercise is to try and see if the total amount of sleep you thought you needed aligns with what your body is trying to communicate to you. There is likely a discrepancy there.

And, if at this point you are thinking, I can't afford to sleep eight hours a day. There is too much to get done and there are not enough hours in the day. I want to assure you that your

Perfectly Productive Day is contingent on you getting a full night of rest.

Do you remember how I struggled with where to start this book because our Perfectly Productive Day is cyclical and reliant on the micro habits and decisions that you make throughout the day? The Perfectly Productive You tomorrow is asking the imperfect you today to give them a little gift, a little favor, a little help in living the Perfectly Productive Day tomorrow. Did that make sense?

So, as you read on and define your bedtime, I encourage you to feel one-hundred percent confident in the length that you have determined to be your perfect amount of sleep. And, even if you decided not to do the suggested experiment of determining the amount of sleep that your body is asking for, I encourage you to add at least thirty minutes to the amount of sleep you are currently getting each night (assuming that length is under eight hours).

Now, let's answer the second question.

What time do you need or want to wake up tomorrow?

To answer this, we need to revisit how we started The Perfectly Productive Day. In the Morning Routine section, we defined the time you need to start work and calculated backward to reach your ideal wake-up time to live your Perfectly Productive Morning.

Sticking with our hypothetical from that section, let's say you need to start work at 8:30 a.m. and, based on the Perfectly Productive Morning that you want to live, you have decided you need to wake up at 6:00 a.m.

You also determined from the first question here that you need eight hours of sleep. (Have I convinced you of that yet?) This means you determined your bedtime to be 10:00 p.m. However, this is not actually your bedtime, and that is where you've been making a mistake.

My good friend Mel Robbins says, "*Your entire Evening Routine depends on this. You have to pick your bedtime. If you don't pick your bedtime, then you do not have an Evening Routine. And that's part of the problem, that most people do not pick a real bedtime. You think, 'Oh, ok, I need to go to bed at 10:00 p.m.' But in reality, you are scrolling until midnight. And so, you have to be intentional about this.*"

Your fall asleep time is when you have finished reading your book, watching your show, or playing games on your phone. This is when you've shut off everything, and you're settling into your favorite pillow and slipping away into dreamland.

In our hypothetical, your bedtime would be some time earlier than 10:00 p.m., so that you are ready to shut your eyes and fall asleep when the clock strikes ten.

In his article for The Atlantic, *The Lie We Tell Ourselves About Going to Bed Early*, Arthur Brooks says,

> "*Thirty minutes prior (to bed), tell yourself, 'I have control over my schedule, and I am choosing to go to bed at this time.'*
>
> *Perhaps this self-talk sounds childish to you, but it's really a way to deal with the situation maturely by quieting your inner squalling toddler.*"

And we've already established that we are all small children in adult bodies.

CHAPTER 16

Setting Up Tomorrow Before You Sleep

Now that we've established your fall asleep time, in this case 10:00 p.m., we need to work backwards to determine what time you should start your Bedtime Routine. What does your Bedtime Routine consist of? What do you need or want to do right before you fall asleep? Some examples might be brushing your teeth, washing your face, reading a book, watching a show in bed, scrolling on social media. What do you need or want to do just before you fall asleep and how long do those activities take?

To help you determine your Perfectly Productive Bedtime Routine, I'll elaborate on mine. At bedtime, I start by washing my face. To be honest, I usually wash my face earlier in the day during the Perfectly Productive Evening Routine whenever possible, but if it hasn't already been done, I do it now. That takes about two minutes.

Kelsey Martin, a Regional Sales Director at Trustmark in the Bay Area, shares a similar nighttime habit:

"Whatever you do, always wash your face and take that makeup off. I actually look forward to it every night! Lately, especially when it's hot, I've been rinsing my feet in cold water to help get my body temperature down and stay cool. We all sleep better when it's cooler."

She's right. Washing your face at night feels refreshing and helps signal to your body that the day is coming to a close.

I promised earlier that I would revisit the idea of changing into your pajamas at this point. While I typically like to do it much earlier in the day, it is not uncommon to wait until The Perfectly Productive Bedtime Routine before you're switching outfits. That's probably what most normal people do. In that case, now is when you'd be taking your workpants off and slipping into those cozy PJs.

This is where I should tell you that I brush my teeth for two minutes, but I am going to be honest and vulnerable here. I don't. I know, I know, it's terrible. I brush my teeth first thing in the morning, but I have developed the non-habit of brushing them at night. While the experts recommend brushing at night, my dentist repeatedly gives me an A on brushing, and so I continue to get away with not doing it at bedtime. But, for the sake of demonstrating the Perfectly Productive Bedtime, let's assume that it would take an additional three minutes here.

Now I crawl into bed and set up my favorite items for my Perfectly Productive Sleep. More on that later. Once in bed, I complete at least one Spanish lesson on Duolingo.

In case you are not familiar with Duolingo, it is a language app, and in my Perfectly Productive Phone exercise, I deemed it a Required app. Duolingo helps me practice speaking Spanish, since my family and I frequently travel to Mexico and have even stayed there for extended summers on a few occasions. As of the time of writing this book, I am on a 926 streak in the app. Each lesson takes an average of two minutes, and typically, I complete two to three lessons per night. So, about five minutes total.

You may be following along and completing the time-math as I am walking you through the Perfectly Productive Bedtime Routine, but if you aren't, I'll get you up to speed. So far, these activities have taken about ten minutes. We haven't even covered what I really like to do once I am settled into the sheets to wind down before sleeping.

After I'm done with Duolingo, I like to do one of two things and sometimes both: either I like to read for a little while, or I like to watch a show on a streaming channel. Either way, I am very clear, at this point, what my *fall asleep* time is, and that means I am very clear on how much time I will do either of those activities.

Going to bed as early as 8:00 p.m., however, is not a requirement for designing your Perfectly Productive Sleep. Sticking with our hypothetical fall asleep time of 10:00 p.m., suppose you started your Perfectly Productive Bedtime Routine at 9:15 p.m. That is when you plug into your Perfectly Productive Evening Routine and transition to the Perfectly Productive Bedtime Routine. You wash your face, brush your teeth, put on your pajamas, and crawl into your bed. It's about 9:28 p.m. at this point (I've added a few minutes as a buffer for any unplanned event that may have leaked some time). This means you have about thirty-two minutes to watch your show, play your games, or read your book.

For some of you reading, you may be thinking: "*This sounds so regimented.*" Or, "*you've got to be kidding me, I have to look at the clock and identify the stop time for my evening activity.*"

Yes.

Look, I am not suggesting this exact level of precision will work for everyone. This, however, is what helps create the

Perfectly Productive Day. Because, without identifying how long you have to read, watch, or play at bedtime, you end up binge-watching well past the 10:00 p.m. fall asleep time. Then you don't get eight hours of sleep. Then you can't get up in the morning to go to the gym, or journal, or read, or enjoy your coffee in a quiet house. Then you are not as productive during the workday. Then you are frustrated and irritated during the evening, and then you are still doing what you've done every day to this point. You're reading this book because you wanted to know how you can live a Perfectly Productive Day, and this is how.

Harvard Medical School published Improving Sleep: A Guide to a Good Night's Rest (you can Google it and purchase the e-book which is chock-full of valuable information extending beyond this book). In that Guide, medical experts state that "a consistent bedtime routine helps you to fall asleep faster and get deeper sleep."

If you don't like the idea of saying "thirty-two minutes EXACTLY," then round it off and provide a range. Say to yourself, "*Okay, I have between twenty and thirty-five minutes to do this bedtime activity I want to do.*" While your bedtime is 10:00 p.m., if it is 9:58 p.m. or 10:04 p.m., that is okay.

Before I digressed, I mentioned that you have *about* thirty-two minutes until…lights out. If you prefer to read as your wind-down activity before falling asleep, then after you finish a chapter or a section of the book, check the clock again to see where you should slip your bookmark in for the night.

Periodically checking the clock will help you gauge whether you can get through one more chapter or section, or if this is a good stopping point. I often do this when I am reading at OrangeTheory® in the morning. When I am at a good stopping point, I'll check the time to see whether I can get through one more section or should place my bookmark now, since the coach is about to announce the start of class. We also explored this a little in the Perfectly Productive Evening Routine when I mentioned that my colleague, Dawn, says she struggles to stop.

Here's the deal. There will always be more to read, more to watch, more to do. You have to know when enough is enough… for now. Eventually, this practice will become a habit and become easier. Give yourself that grace to practice this new routine of stopping, even when you do not want to. Being Perfectly Productive is often about doing and getting things done, but it is equally about stopping and aligning with the feeling that this is enough for today.

The same thing applies to watching something during your Bedtime Routine. We live in a society where things are easily available, and we can always get more. We can order something, and it can arrive on our doorstep within minutes or hours. We finish watching a short clip, and the next one starts playing automatically. We finish a series, and fifteen more are waiting to be started. We have more books on our digital bookshelf than we could read in a lifetime. We always want more.

I liked what Katie said about her binge watching, "*both are very good (shows), but neither disappearing off the platform any time soon (or probably ever).*"

Sometimes…we need to settle for less to gain more in other areas. Watching less at bedtime will help you gain more time throughout your day and will help you be the Perfectly Productive You that you and I both know you're capable of.

We discussed this in the Perfectly Productive Evening Routine, but let's remind ourselves of the strategy. You have approximately thirty-two minutes until you need to stop and begin to fall asleep. Typically, I check how much time is left in the episode so I can decide whether to watch it in full. Suppose my current show has thirty-seven minutes left. In that case, I will likely decide to watch it. After all, thirty-two minutes is not exact, and typically, the last few minutes are credits anyway. Great, I begin watching with an understanding that at the end of this episode, I will pause and hold onto the suspense until tomorrow.

Let's say the show is an hour long. Now I have the information that I need to make a decision. Do I want to watch something else so I don't have to stop the episode in the middle? Or am I ok with stopping in the middle?

Stopping in the middle of an episode usually doesn't bother me, but maybe it would for you. Know yourself and your preferences and limits, and it will help you decide what will work for you. Just plan ahead, because a failure to plan is a plan to fail… tomorrow.

Since my Perfectly Productive Morning Routine means that I am waking up at 4:30 a.m., and because I've identified that I prefer eight hours of sleep, this means that my fall asleep time is about 8:30 p.m. Usually, I start my Perfectly Productive Bedtime Routine around 7:45 to 8:00 p.m. and adjust my reading or watching time to align with falling asleep around 8:30 p.m.

Research has found that watching a show or doing an activity on your phone immediately before bed will impact your sleep. You may have already been thinking that, as I've outlined a Perfectly Productive Bedtime Routine to include an activity on your phone. That's counterintuitive, since this book is about being Perfectly Productive, and yet you know you shouldn't be on your phone in bed. In fact, your phone should be in a different room from your bedroom. We covered this during the Perfectly Productive Morning Routine.

A few important things to note at this point about my habit of watching something before bed. It works for me because I don't check my phone at all during the night. I also don't hit snooze in the morning, which means I don't need to place my phone in another room just to force myself out of bed. And finally, I use an automatic blue light setting on my phone.

At 8:00 p.m., my phone switches into blue light mode and stays there until 5:00 a.m. Research shows that screen use before bed can affect sleep, but it also points to blue light as the more significant factor. Managing that exposure has made a meaningful difference for me.

The takeaway here isn't whether your phone can eventually live next to your bed. It's those habits that are built through small, intentional changes. As you work through the practices in this book, you may reach a place where your phone no longer interferes with your sleep. You'll know when to stop for the night, whether that's 10:00 p.m. or another time that works for you, and you'll sleep soundly for the hours your body needs.

For now, however, your phone may need to live in a different room. Not as a punishment, but as a practical boundary that protects your rest and keeps old, unproductive habits from creeping back in. Think of it this way: you're not being punished. The phone is simply being put in its place.

We've discussed a few activities to do, or not do, to help you wind down and fall asleep at night. If you're struggling to fall asleep, consider that the phone, television, or reading might be keeping you up, and perhaps take a bath instead.

Dr. Gina Poe is a well-known UCLA neuroscientist who researches sleep and routines. She emphasizes that a consistent bedtime, aligned with your body's circadian rhythm, is crucial—not just for deep sleep, but also for releasing growth hormones and supporting brain cleaning functions. Dr. Poe also finds that a healthy wind-down or bedtime routine often includes calming rituals like taking a warm bath, which can help initiate natural sleep by signaling your body that it's time to wind down.

When it is time for our children to Go the F--k to Sleep, we often encourage them to wind down. We ask them to brush their teeth, turn off electronics, and maybe even take a bath. Yet when it comes to our adult selves, we think we can just shut down by hitting the lock button on our phones or powering off the television. Our mind doesn't work that way. Remember, we are really high-functioning toddlers. Investing in a wind-down ritual will help you fall asleep faster and kick-start the Perfectly Productive You tomorrow.

At the end of each day, Dr. Daniel Amens embarks on a treasure hunt from his day. Dr. Amen is an American celebrity doctor who practices as a psychiatrist and brain disorder specialist. He emphasizes the power of mindset in shaping your day, and by reflecting on "what went well?"

Answering this question helps him wire his brain with positive thoughts and embark on an expedition to find the gold nuggets of his day.

Try it. It will train your brain to find and appreciate micro-moments of joy, such as spotting hummingbirds or butterflies. It fosters gratitude, rewires your brain for positivity, and sets the foundation for a fulfilling life. And, Dr. Amen reports that it helps him fall asleep. As he explores "what went well," there are nights that he follows a long list of answers to that question. There are also nights when he responds with one or two things…and then falls into dreamland quickly.

The Perfectly Productive Day is not about being perfect. It is about finding what works perfectly for you and developing systems, habits, and routines to be consistent whenever possible.

And now it's time for you to go and find your bedtime mathematical formula and design your Perfectly Productive Sleep before it hijacks you.

When Martha Wins

On a particular night, when I should have been winding down and going to bed, I checked LinkedIn posts. That was when I saw Katie Burke's post recommending Martha on Netflix.

Perfect timing. I had about thirty minutes until bedtime, and I needed a new show to watch. Katie's enthusiastic recommendation for the short series led me to hit play. Thanks, Katie.

I got sucked in.

I should have gone to bed at 8:30 p.m. since I needed to be up at 4:30 a.m. for the gym. In fact, most nights, no matter how exciting or dramatic my show or book is, I stop that activity at 8:30 p.m. to honor my Perfectly Productive Bedtime Routine since it provides the beautiful gift to the Tomorrow Me that we have extensively spoken about in this book.

But, on this particular night, I ignored my own wisdom and advice. I failed myself, and I could not stop watching. In fact, the Introduction of this book is about this particular night.

I did not watch the entire show. Eventually, I got too tired and stopped. But I went well beyond 8:30 p.m.

That led me to turn off my alarm at 4:30 a.m. the next day.

And that decision led to not going to the gym the next morning.

And that decision led to decision fatigue the next day, when I couldn't decide what time to squeeze in my workout. Which resulted in me not going to the gym and blaming myself. Which probably led to doom scrolling the next night.

You see how this is all tying together now?

And as I hope we have learned together, while we discuss what the formula might be for your Perfectly Productive Day, I want you to understand that it is not expected that you live this Perfectly Productive Day every day. Just like I don't. Stuff happens. We make choices in the moment – productive or not. And that's ok.

I said a few paragraphs ago that "I failed myself." As I am writing this, I was going to go back and edit that part out. Instead, I decided to keep it in because I want you to see how the negative self-talk and the limiting beliefs play out in real time.

My first thought as I was writing this was to say, "I failed myself," because my choice and my actions the night before meant I couldn't wake up the next morning.

I did not fail.

We are working together here to change our narrative about ourselves and reduce the negative self-talk. I did not fail. I decided that night to enjoy more of Martha, at the cost of deciding the gym was not a priority for me the next morning. It was a choice, not a failure.

Just like your choices, actions, and decisions are just that. They happened. We are not here to judge ourselves or each other. We are here to feel excited and empowered that we get to make choices and decisions. And to understand what choices and decisions are most often the healthiest and most productive for who we know ourselves to be.

I know that my best and most productive self is the one who goes to bed at 8:30 p.m. and wakes up at 4:30 a.m. Many days, I am that person.

Many days, I am not. And that's ok. I forgive myself for the days I made a different decision. It happened, and I moved on – resetting to my Perfectly Productive self again at the first opportunity the next day.

The average person experiences four thousand weeks in their lifetime. That's 28,000 days and nights. Does the number of days in your life surprise you? Does it seem like a lot? Or not enough? I am not sure I truly conceptualize that number.

Even at the prime of your life, where you sit today, you still have many days ahead of you to make some of them Perfectly Productive….and to be content with all of them, no matter how they get defined at the end of them.

Now, let's get a good night's sleep so that Tomorrow-You is set up for success.

Sleep Routine

....

"Your future depends on your dreams, so go to sleep."

- MESUT BARAZANY

CHAPTER 17

Settling the Mind
Before Sleep

During the time that I was writing this book, I started to see a hypnotherapist. Up until this point in my life, I did not have much interest in seeking out hypnotherapy. It was suggested to me to explore a back spasm that I have during massages to see if there is trauma stuck in that muscle. Quite early in the hypnotherapy sessions, my subconscious said that the back spasms weren't a concern, and, apparently, I did not want to explore that potential trauma.

Instead, I was interested in exploring my creativity for writing this book. In the second session, my hypnotherapist led me on a journey to find my creativity. She led me on a long journey up a hill and into a large, beautiful building with an expansive library. On the second floor, books lined the glass walls overlooking the stunning ocean landscape. All the books in this library were unfinished stories waiting for their authors. On the shelf, I saw my book, *The Perfectly Productive Day*. Seeing it there was the nudge I needed to finish creating and ultimately producing this book.

Patience in the Pause Before Slumber

I am describing this scene now because this imagery has been beneficial for my creativity in writing this book and has also helped me fall asleep.

Often, when I turn off my Netflix show or put down my book, and I am ready to fall asleep, it takes time before I am truly off to dreamland. Typically, this process takes anywhere from five to twenty minutes. I used to think that meant I wasn't tired, or that I wasn't overly tired, or that it meant I *should* be reading more or watching more Netflix.

It's not.

Dr. Rebecca Robbins is an Assistant Professor of Medicine at Brigham and Women's Hospital in Massachusetts and an expert on sleep. Her research finds that it is normal for it to take some time to fall asleep. Dr. Robbins says that a mistake many of us make is believing that to get eight hours of sleep, we need to go to bed eight hours before we wake up.

Dr. Robbins finds that even the best sleepers usually take about twenty minutes to truly fall asleep. In fact, according to *Improving Sleep: A Guide to a Good Night's Rest*, by Harvard Medical School, a forty-year-old individual should take about seventeen minutes to fall asleep. A sixty-year-old will take about eighteen minutes, a seventy-year-old will take about eighteen and a half minutes, and an eighty-year-old might take nineteen minutes to fall asleep.

If you are falling asleep too quickly, it is likely that you've had too much to drink or you have extended yourself past the point of exhaustion. That will lead to poor sleep later in the night.

Stories that Send You to Sleep

According to The Sleep Research Society, sleep influences nearly all of the body's molecular, cellular, physiological, and neurobehavioral processes. In other words, sleep – good and restful sleep – is essential for our health, wellbeing, and productivity.

While you are sleeping, your body, mind, and brain are more active than when you are awake. While you sleep, your brain consolidates and cements your memories and events into long-term storage.

When you feel behind or like you have too much to do, you believe that, instead of sleeping, tapping into those late hours will be productive and beneficial. The opposite is true. This pattern leads to more mistakes, decreased creativity, inefficiencies, increased stress, and overall poorer work product.

According to the CDC, about 70 million Americans have chronic sleep problems. And if you are in that group, falling asleep does not always come quickly or easily. Since it can take a few minutes to up to twenty minutes to fall asleep, we sometimes need to do something meditative to pass the time. Revisiting the journey to my creative studio taps into the right side of my brain, the creative side, and it also helps me to fall asleep.

There are two reasons that reliving this story in my mind helps me to fall asleep. First, it is because of the journey itself. When I slow down and start to put myself back on the trail leading up to the library, then I again feel my body take each step meticulously and intentionally, and before I know it, I am asleep. It's almost like I bore myself to sleep.

The other reason I think reliving that story works is that my subconscious mind is what created the journey to the library of unfinished stories. And to fully invest in the story, my subconscious mind plays an integral role. That activation allows my conscious mind to pass the torch to my subconscious, putting me into a deep sleep. Normally, when I replay this journey in my mind at sleep time, I barely make it to the building before I am fast asleep. It really works.

I am challenging and encouraging you to think of a story you can return to over and over. It could be something that really happened to you, and you want to replay the events of that day. Perhaps something like your wedding day, your kids' graduation from elementary school, or an incredible vacation you took. I'd recommend thinking about a pleasant story or something that brings positive memories, rather than something that happened and is upsetting. If you can't think of anything, I have a few suggestions that may work for you.

Interviewing the Invisible Counselors

In his book *Think and Grow Rich*, Napoleon Hill describes a technique where he would hold an imaginary council meeting with what he called his "Invisible Counselors" just before going to sleep.

Just before falling asleep, Hill would choose nine individuals he admired, including historical and contemporary figures such as Thomas Paine, Ralph Waldo Emerson, Thomas Edison, Charles Darwin, Abraham Lincoln, and Henry Ford.

He would then speak to them in his imagination. The nightly repetition and strong emotional connection with this visualization were designed to impress Hill's subconscious mind. This was done to "rebuild his own character" by internalizing the counselors' combined wisdom and traits, and to help him fall asleep.

He says, "*You cannot entirely control your subconscious mind, but you can voluntarily hand over to it any plan, desire, or purpose which you wish transformed into concrete form.*"

Can you think of five individuals whom you personally consider as someone you admire, respect, or aspire to be? For example, you might think of your grandfather, Maya Angelou, Oprah, the man on your train in a fedora, or the Dalai Lama.

Now, imagine each of them sitting around a large table together. Every night, you walk into that room, and you imagine those five people. One by one, you go through them and ask each the same question. It can be any question; the important thing is that you keep them in the same order and ask the same question.

Some nights, you might make it through all five of your identified figures. Other nights, you might barely make it past the first person. Either way, this habit, the repetition, and the requirement to tap into your subconscious will help you fall asleep quicker.

Try it and tell me what you think.

Counting Backwards

Using imagery is one technique to help you fall asleep. Another technique that I often use is counting backwards from ninety-nine. When I use this technique, I play a game that goes like this.

Starting at ninety-nine, I fully visualize that number in my mind, then count backward.

Ninety-nine.

Ninety-eight.

Ninety-seven.

Ninety-six.

When my mind begins to wander from the visual of the number to something unrelated — which it often does, and it will — I start back at the top, at ninety-nine.

At the beginning of the game each night, I will often get to a number in the nineties before my mind wanders. It's annoying. I'll get to ninety-five, for example, and then have to go back up to Ninety-nine.

Then, I'll make it to the eighties.

Then, eventually, the seventies.

Until, well, until I don't remember anymore. Because I'm asleep.

There are some nights I have made it to count all the way to the thirties. Those nights feel terrible because if I've made it that far, it feels as though I'll never get to sleep. But here's the deal: I don't recall ever having made it to zero.

Which demonstrates that, while incredibly boring, counting backwards is also incredibly effective. Try it.

CHAPTER 18

Creating the Right Conditions for Rest

We've discussed some techniques that will help you fall asleep, and now we will discuss getting the Perfectly Productive Sleep to help round out your Perfectly Productive Day.

There is a catchy Expedia commercial called *"Made to Travel: Insomnia."*

The advertisement opens with a woman, Kiko, sleeping on a boat while her companion, seemingly her husband, reads a book. Next, she sleeps by the pool while he swims, and then she is seen lying sprawled on the grass as he enjoys the ocean view.

The narrator says,

> *"Kiko thought she was an insomniac. But actually, she is just a workaholic."*

It's a creative, entertaining, and realistic commercial that encourages and reminds you to book a vacation.

If you haven't already discovered how many hours your body is truly craving for sleep, I'd recommend you invest the time into that exercise now – or visit Expedia to book a trip to invest in this research.

We established in the Perfectly Productive Bedtime Routine that you should aim to get about eight hours of sleep per night, unless you've done the week-long sleep test and found that you truly do not need that much time.

Experts, however, suggest that seven to nine hours of sleep per night for the average adult is preferable and advised.

We also recognized that your bedtime is not when you fall asleep. In fact, you should be starting your Perfectly Productive Bedtime Routine probably thirty minutes to an hour before you plan on falling asleep.

Now, let's explore what the Perfectly Productive Sleep environment might look like for you in order to ensure you are getting the recommended seven to nine hours of uninterrupted sleep and, ideally, cycling through five circadian rhythms.

Confessions of a Sleep Diva

Here is where I am going to admit something a little embarrassing. Well, another embarrassing thing about me, since there were a few of them in the book.

I am a Sleep Diva.

Yes, it's true. I am not someone, anymore, who can lay my head down anywhere and fall asleep.

I used to be able to do so. Over the years, I have added things to my Perfectly Productive Sleep Routine. When I was in college, I remember my roommate telling me she had to sleep with the fan on and confirming it wouldn't bother me. It wouldn't, I told her.

Now, we are not talking about a small and quiet fan. She had a fan so large and so loud that I am pretty sure it was a refabricated airplane engine. Our shared room sounded like you were trying to sleep in a wind tunnel. Fortunately, I could sleep through the noise, and in college, I did not need any tools to fall asleep.

As I have aged, I have added a few necessities to achieve Perfectly Productive Sleep.

First, my sheets have to be tucked in. We are talking about hotel/nurse's corners that guarantee that I am wrapped tighter than a burrito at night. I need to be able to move my foot to the edge and hit the guardrails that are my sheets nailed under the mattress.

While I have always appreciated a dark room for sleeping, I eventually added a tight eye mask to improve sleep. For many years, that was my only add-on in my sleep divaness.

Then, years later, I started to put a pillow over my head. Each night, I would crawl into my tightly tucked sheets and put the comforter over my body. Then, I'd put my eye mask over my eyes, and my head would be sandwiched between two pillows.

About six years ago, my dentist recommended a night guard for me to mitigate the clenching that I was doing at night. That suggestion by my dentist has proven to be clutch for me. I cannot sleep well without it. I know I am not alone, and there are a few of us out there. Nightguard Users Unite!

My Perfectly Productive Sleep used to include sheets tucked in tight, an eye mask, a nightguard in my mouth, a dark room, and pillows on either side of my head when I fell asleep on my side.

As if that weren't enough, over the past year, I started putting earplugs in my ears on many nights. This started because we rescued a dog who howls in the middle of the night. Not quite awake, she will sit up, extend her neck, and howl at an octave that is deafening. Nobody would be able to sleep through it. It often wakes my sons up…two rooms away. Before we rescued her, she was an outside dog, and her howling would wake up neighbors, who later warned me about it when we rescued her from the neighborhood. Because it is inconsistent and very distracting, I started wearing earplugs to reduce its impact on my Perfectly Productive Sleep. Hence, adding another need to my sleep routine.

Very recently, my son bought me a stuffed animal octopus. I have a minor obsession with octopuses, and he saw this stuffed animal when we were on a trip. It is designed for a baby or toddler and even has a rattle inside of it. Well, I started to snuggle with the octopus when I would settle into my pre-sleep dream story. His large, round head is the perfect size for me to cup my hand around. And while the octopus is a newer addition in the last month of writing this section, I am afraid it might be here to stay.

To recap, my Perfectly Productive Sleep is quite dramatic and needy. Every night, my Perfectly Productive Bedtime Routine means that I am:

- Ensuring the sheets are tucked in tightly.
- Putting my nightguard into my mouth.
- Putting the sleep mask over my head.
- Ensuring a second pillow is nearby to put over my head when the lights go out.
- Tucking my octopus nearby to cuddle with.
- Sometimes I put the earplugs into my ears.
- Oh, and taking my evening medication (which I did not mention above).

And if you're wondering how I adjust when I am traveling, the answer is…I don't. The nightguard, earplugs, and eye mask are brought along with me. Hotels almost always have enough pillows that I can claim two. The question is whether to bring the octopus at this point, and that is still to be determined.

Given my Perfectly Productive Sleep additions over the last ten or so years, by the time I am eighty years old, I am going to need gloves, a sleep sack, and a pacifier to get into a Perfectly Productive Sleep. I am kidding…I hope.

What Support Do You Need for Your Perfectly Productive Sleep?

Maryann Reyes, a CPA in Florida and a Partner at the international accounting firm Withum, says her Perfectly Productive Day means she gets a good night's sleep. I completely agree with her, which is why I've created and expanded my sleep routine.

What, if anything, do you need to fall into your Perfectly Productive Sleep?

I am not suggesting you create an environment that requires as much stuff as mine does; however, Dr. Rebecca Robbins's research has shown that it may take you some time to fall asleep. If you fall asleep quickly, it is likely because you have formed habits that may not be the best sleep habits. Whether it is a caffeine crash, a buzzed slumber, being overly exhausted, or using medicines to speed up the process. Additionally, if you are not falling asleep quickly enough, you may need to adjust your bedtime or the tools you use to help you fall asleep within roughly fifteen to twenty minutes.

Sarah Spector is a CPA in Walnut Creek, California, and the owner of Spector Wellman CPA firm. For a few months now, Sarah has been struggling to fall asleep, which, of course, means that she is often not getting the length and quality of sleep that her body craves.

She also recognizes that this challenge is not only affecting the hours of rest she needs but also her goals and productivity for the next day.

Sarah's Perfectly Productive Day starts with journaling in the morning. She finds that thirty minutes of writing each morning helps her clear her mind, set and follow her goals, and get started on the right foot the next day. Her current struggles to fall asleep are affecting her Morning Routine, which in turn is affecting her Workday and Evening Routine.

For the past few days, Sarah has been taking Tylenol PM to help her body reset. She has found that doing so for three nights is like sleep training her body. After those three nights, her body recognizes what it should be doing and falls asleep more quickly on its own.

Let's see if we can identify what your Perfectly Productive Sleep needs. One way to determine this is to think about the last time you slept in a room that was not your own – such as a hotel room or a friend's house. Assuming a drunken sleep wasn't at play – because let's be real, sleeping in a hotel often means that it is – then I want you to think about the sleep you had.

Was it the best night of sleep you've had in a long time? Why? Was it because the room was dark? Was it tightly tucked in sheets? Was it because you didn't have other noises around you that have been normalized at home? Was it their high-thread-count sheets? Did you use their complimentary eye mask or earplugs?

Similarly, was it a terrible night of sleep? Why? Perhaps the room was too cold…or too hot. Did you hear people walking by all night, suggesting you're sensitive to unfamiliar sounds? Were the sheets tucked in too tightly? Did the pillows suck?

That insight might help you identify small changes you can make in your bedroom to support Perfectly Productive Sleep.

Identify what they are and then make small changes to see if your sleep improves.

If you haven't been to a hotel in a while, maybe this is your sign to book a staycation, grab a new book (because you are almost done with this one), and enjoy a day alone and all to yourself.

Release Today, Restore Tomorrow

"Finish each day and be done with it. You have done what you could." Ralph Waldo Emerson, the great American philosopher, wrote this in a letter to his daughter who was worried about a mistake she had made.

Why is it that our brain decides sleep time is the best time to ruminate?

Probably because it is the first opportunity in the day to just stop and think. The first opportunity to quiet our minds from the busyness of the day, and then our thoughts become active.

Yet, worrying about things does not prove helpful, beneficial, or productive.

Ralph Waldo Emerson continues the letter with, *"Some blunders, losses, and absurdities no doubt crept in; forget them as soon as you can."*

Jason Wilson is the author of *The Man the Moment Demands* and a longtime mentor to boys and men. Jason created for himself the concept of the four R's: reflect, release, reset, and rest.

Jason says that to truly protect his rest, he stopped allowing the disappointments of the day to follow him into the night. He reminds himself that tomorrow is what unfinished work is for, and there is nothing more he can do with today's problems once the day is over. Instead, he reflects, releases, resets, and then rests.

One simple way to support this release is to write down the swirling thoughts and lingering to-dos that often surface just as your head hits the pillow. Externalizing what's unfinished gives your mind a clear place to put it, signaling that it's safe to disengage for the night.

This practice is supported by research. Psychologists E. J. Masicampo and Roy F. Baumeister found that writing down unfinished tasks is more cognitively beneficial than listing completed ones. In their study, *"Consider It Done!"*, participants who captured incomplete tasks—especially when paired with a simple plan—experienced fewer intrusive thoughts and a reduced mental load. The act of documenting open tasks effectively signaled to the brain that the work was contained, allowing it to rest more fully at the end of the day.

Furthermore, *Improving Sleep: A Guide to a Good Night's Rest* by Harvard Medical School states:

> *"Worrying about a problem or a long To-Do list can be a recipe for insomnia. Well, before you turn in, try writing down your worries and make a list of tasks you want to remember. This "worry journal" may help move these distracting thoughts from your mind."*

Now, if you're still developing your Trusted System at work, consider the simple suggestion by Harvard Medical School. Start a "worry journal" and keep that near where you settle in for your Perfectly Productive Evening Routine. Instead of the doom scrolling or the binge watching, instead, journal in your "worry journal" and watch your sleep improve!

Understanding the Science of Sleep

Most people think of sleep as a single event. You go to bed. You fall asleep. You wake up.

But sleep doesn't work that way.

Sleep is a process that runs in cycles of about 90 minutes each, much like a washing machine running through its programmed sequence.

You don't press "start" and get clean clothes instantly. The machine moves through different cycles, each one doing a specific job. If you miss a cycle or cut it short, the clothes won't be fully cleaned or ready to go!

Your brain and body work the same way while you sleep. Your brain and body run through cycles so that you, too, are ready to go. Let us geek out for just a little bit about the sleep cycles we experience during our Perfectly Productive Sleep.

One of the simplest ways I've discovered to explain sleep, is to think of it like your washing machine's full program. When you put clothes into a washing machine, it doesn't clean them all at once. It moves through a series of cycles that repeat through-out the full wash. I'm sure you've heard it.

Your night of sleep follows a pattern in which it cycles through light sleep, deep sleep, and dream sleep about four to five times per night.

Each cycle has a purpose, and each one matters.

Light Sleep: The Pre-Wash and Soak Cycle (50% of Your Night)

This is where the machine is filled with water and begins its gentle motion. There is nothing intense yet, but everything is being prepared. Surprisingly, just like the pre-wash takes up a good chunk of the total wash time, you'll spend about half your night here in light sleep.

In your body:

- Your breathing and heart rate slow down
- Your brain waves shift from alert to relaxed
- Your temperature begins to drop
- Your muscles start to release tension

Opening the washing machine during pre-wash won't ruin anything, but it stops the process; similarly, light sleep is easy to interrupt. A sound, a light, even a familiar whisper of your name can pull you right back out of light sleep. You've experi-enced this before when you're suddenly awake, even slightly, and you question whether you had ever been asleep at all.

What this cycle does: Light sleep transitions you from awake to asleep and acts as the bridge between sleep cycles all night long. Light sleep is certainly not wasted time, as your brain is actually organizing memories and disconnecting from the outside world. Pretty cool, huh? Then we enter deep sleep.

Deep Sleep: The Heavy-Duty Power Wash (20% of Your Night)

This is where the real cleaning happens.

The washing machine shifts into its strongest cycle during this heavy-duty power wash. The drum spins with purpose, and even the toughest stains get knocked loose. You couldn't stop this cycle easily if you tried. This is what happens to your brain and body during deep sleep.

In your body:

- Blood pressure drops by 20-30%
- Growth hormone floods your system
- Muscles and tissues repair
- Your immune system goes into overdrive
- Brain waves slow to their deepest rhythm

This is physical restoration at full power. It's nearly impossible to wake someone from deep sleep, and if you do, they'll feel groggy and disoriented, like clothes pulled out mid-wash.

What this cycle does: Deep sleep is when your body does its heavy maintenance work. This is why athletes need extra deep sleep for recovery, and why you feel physically drained without it. (Note: After age 65, deep sleep naturally decreases, which is why older adults often feel less physically restored.)

Dream Sleep: The Rinse and Spin Cycle (25% of Your Night)

After the heavy wash, comes the rinse and spin, which removes what's left behind and prepares everything for use.

Dream sleep is actually your most active sleep stage. Your brain lights up like it's awake, but your body is essentially paralyzed (except for your darting eyes). It's like the spin cycle – intense activity with a specific purpose.

In your brain:

- Yesterday's experiences get filed into long-term memory
- Emotions are processed and regulated
- Creative connections are made
- Problem-solving pathways are strengthened
- Stress hormones are cleared out

What this cycle does: Dream sleep restores your mind the way deep sleep restores your body. Without entering this state, or staying there long enough, you will wake up mentally foggy, emotionally raw, and less able to handle complex tasks. This is true even if you have got plenty of hours in bed.

The Complete Overnight Program

Here's what most people don't realize: these cycles repeat and evolve throughout the night. Earlier in the night, you will experience deep sleep (heavy washing when clothes are dirtiest).

Later in the night, you enter dream sleep (extra rinse cycles to ensure everything's clear).

Each 90-minute cycle covers all the stages, but the proportions change. If you miss the early cycles, you lose deep sleep, and that leads to the Perfectly Unproductive Morning. When you cut your night short and you miss the extended dream periods, you will feel like you need extra caffeine to get through your Perfectly Productive Workday.

If you wear a watch to bed that tracks your sleep, these cycles might make a little more sense now.

When you constantly wake up, go to bed late, or set an early alarm, it's like repeatedly stopping the washing machine mid-cycle.

The clothes are wet. They smell off. They're not ready to wear. This is why someone can be "in bed" for eight hours but feel exhausted. You now know that you need the uninterrupted 90-minute sequences to run their course.

The Bottom Line: Let the Full Program Run

You don't need to understand the intricate science behind sleep to benefit from it. You just need to respect the process and how it benefits your productivity throughout the day.

Give your body enough time to run the full program and to experience multiple 90-minute cycles. Determine your bedtime mathematical formula, reduce interruptions, and lean into your sleep divaness. Then, let each stage do its job. Create the conditions that allow the full program to run.

When you do, you wake up truly restored with your body repaired, your mind clear, and ready for the Perfectly Productive Tomorrow You.

Because quality sleep isn't about logging hours. It's about completing cycles.

CHAPTER 20

When Sleep Doesn't Go as Planned

You and I are working on your sleep, so you may already be noticing a positive difference in how you sleep. Chances are, however, you will still wake up at night. The Harvard Medical School's *Improving Sleep: A Guide to a Good Night's Rest* states:

> *"In older adults…falling asleep takes longer, and the shallow quality of sleep results in dozens of awakenings during the night."*

Even if you do everything perfectly, there are certainly nights that you will not have Perfectly Productive Sleep. It happens to all of us. I have a technique that helps me fall back to sleep in the middle of the night, and I want to share it with you.

Like you, there are times I wake up in the middle of the night, and my mind is immediately flooded with a lot of random thoughts and To-Dos. My head fills as though it is a Main Street at Disneyland – over-crowded, noisy, and congested. In that moment, I try to push those random thoughts aside to get the image of a dark space. Slowly, meticulously, and intentionally, I draw up a black space. Once the space is as dark and as scarce as possible, I start to envision myself as a cartoon woman.

This image doesn't have to be a cartoon character; in fact, it probably doesn't even necessarily need to be you specifically. But it needs to be an image of a person or animal that can help you capture these random thoughts.

Once the image is very clear, and I am standing alone in the dark room, I picture my cartoon self holding a net. At this time, if the thoughts are trying to enter the room, I work really hard to push them temporarily to the side of the room, like you are squeezing them out. Assure those thoughts that in just a minute, they will be welcomed back into the room.

Next to the cartoon character of myself holding the net is a box. It could be a cardboard box or a cute little woven box. It is closed and has a small chute attached.

Once the image of myself holding a net and with a box next to me is clear, I then release the hold on the random thoughts and invite them into the room.

The thoughts, ideas, and To-Dos start flooding in and filling the black space in my mind. The cartoon version of me starts to fly around the room, taking her net and capturing those Butterfly Thoughts and putting them in the box through the chute. I call them Butterfly Thoughts because they are flying around like little butterflies, and butterflies do not belong out and about at night – and neither do those random thoughts you have.

As more Butterfly Thoughts come flooding in, I watch myself grab the net and capture that next round of thoughts. I open a chute attached to the box, and I put the rest of those thoughts into the box through the chute. This continues for a few rounds until it is evident that I've captured most of the random thoughts in my head. My brain starts to clear up and become quieter.

If I haven't already fallen asleep, because sometimes I have, then at this point, I realize that the thoughts start to become less frequent. Most of those Butterfly Thoughts are now captured in my box. The box is not garbage or waste; those thoughts are not discounted or thrown away, they are simply stored away safely for another time.

Now, my mind is quiet, and one random thought will come flying into the space. That random Butterfly Thought is likely the one that was really keeping me awake to begin with. It is the most important thought.

Maybe it is to mail a card or a birthday present. Maybe it is to respond to a potential client. Maybe it is a project that I am very aware of and have been procrastinating on. Maybe it is that I haven't done the dishes from last night's dinner. Whatever it is, that Butterfly Thought will become very clear because it surfaced after all of the noise has been mitigated.

Now that I have identified the important Butterfly Thought, there are a few healthy things to do with it. Naturally, you may want to get up and do the thing; however, in most cases, that is not advised. Whatever it is, if you get up and do it, it will stimulate you and fully activate your conscious mind, making it increasingly difficult to fall back asleep.

Instead, have a notebook near your bed to jot down the Butterfly Thought – maybe it's the worry journal we just discussed. Using your phone is not advised because the light will wake you, and you could easily get sucked into the notifications awaiting you.

Writing the Butterfly Thought down on a small notepad – or your *Worry Journal* – next to your bed is the best practice. Then, in the morning, make it a habit to check your small notepad and rip out the page that contains the Butterfly Thought. Either complete that task as soon as you have the opportunity, or add it to your Trusted System (your To-Do list).

Often, I do not need to write down the Butterfly Thought because I can identify another trigger or reminder to complete the task the next day. For example, suppose I woke up in the night and thought, "I need to check in with my client, Lisa, about the project she was working on and whether she started the research on it."

I don't want to forget to check in with Lisa, but this Butterfly Thought isolated itself in the middle of the night. I am not going to check in with Lisa in the middle of the night. I could write it down, but even writing it down will sometimes awaken me more than I'd like.

Instead, I remember that Lisa's client file is sitting on my desk because I need to process her payment tomorrow. I will create a connecting thought in that moment:

When I see Lisa's file folder tomorrow, don't forget to send her an email to check in on her project's research.

Then I am able to fall back asleep.

Recognize, however, that you have to know yourself and whether the Tomorrow You would still recall the connection between seeing her file folder and knowing to reach out to her to check in.

For example, Michele Day, a CPA from Danville, California, says that,

> "*I keep a notepad by my bed to write down ideas that come to mind at night. Or pose a question to the Universe before going to sleep, and have that question waiting for me the next morning. Being aware that the Universe always gives me exactly what I need and exactly when I need it. Often, I see the answer when I stop to look.*"

That's powerful stuff, Michele.

My technique of linking the Butterfly Thought to a trigger has helped me on many nights when I wake up, and my mind is thinking about something that does not matter, like a butterfly that should not be flying around in the middle of the night. The Butterfly Thoughts are valuable, they're interesting, they're important, and in some cases, you might even describe them as beautiful. But, like butterflies should not be active in the night, neither should your random thoughts.

And if you know yourself and you know that you will reach for your phone in the middle of the night. Well, then you need to use tools and systems to be more productive and to break that bad habit.

Forming new habits is quite simple when you define the trigger, the action, and the reward. Then, make the things you want to do easy, and the things you do not want to do difficult.

Right now, grabbing your phone at night is too easy. Make it difficult. Like Anne Sharp, who you met earlier – a CPO®

from Boston, Massachusetts. Anne says she charges her phone in the kitchen overnight so she isn't tempted to check it at night.

Super smart, Anne.

And sometimes we have those nights when the butterflies won't settle, and the brain waves are fully awake and functioning. Let's explore what the Perfectly Productive You will do on those nights.

Still Can't Sleep – Then Get Up!

As a middle-aged woman who overall sleeps well, I thought I had sleep solved. At least I thought that in the last few years, I've learned a lot about what I need for a Perfectly Productive Sleep. In short, I know I need eight to nine hours per night. I know I need time to fall asleep. I know that I hate to be interrupted in the night by anything – the kids, the dog, the Butterfly Thoughts. And I thought that, when I couldn't sleep, I should just continue to try, even if it meant tossing and turning a few times.

Wrong.

Dr. Robbins, the sleep expert we met earlier, recommends that if you cannot fall back asleep, you should get up and out of bed. That's crazy, I used to think. Why would I get up when the chances of falling back to sleep are zero percent? Versus at least trying to fall back asleep, there is some likelihood that it will occur.

What Dr. Robbins says is that we should train our brains to associate our bed with comfort and sleep. Well, and maybe one other thing, but that's not what this book is about. Comfort and sleep.

When you wake up in the middle of the night and you are not able to fall back to sleep, continuing to fight it confuses your mind into thinking that your bed is a place of anxiety, stress, and discomfort. It makes sense, doesn't it?

Instead, Dr. Robbins recommends that if you can't sleep for an extended period of time, then you should get up.

Maybe you already do that – get up, that is – but you may be doing the rest of it all wrong.

Dr. Robbins says that when you can't sleep, you should get up and do something that is productive, tedious, and maybe a bit boring. Do not get up and watch television, scroll on social media, or work. That will awaken your senses and create an emotional response that makes it difficult to fall back asleep when you return to your bed. (Not to mention start to train yourself to get into the habit of waking each night.)

Instead, Dr. Robbins recommends activities such as organizing a drawer, folding socks, working on a jigsaw puzzle, reading, or engaging in a low-stimulating activity.

I'm about to be very vulnerable here, but I want to be honest and helpful. I am a middle-aged white woman experiencing perimenopause (sorry, TMI), and recently I have been suffering from restless leg syndrome (RLS) and internal tremors. The first night I had RLS, I had no choice but to get up because the discomfort from the restless legs was ruthless, and I needed to move my legs. Now that I've heard Dr. Robbins's research and recommendations, I know that getting up is the right thing to do.

My youngest son and I are working on a small side business together in which we rent Legos® to nearby families. This initiative means I am organizing Legos®, updating inventory for Lego® sets, and packaging them in my free time. It's tedious, maybe a little boring, and ultimately productive since it helps my business. Honestly, if I could organize Legos® as a full-time job, I probably would. I love it. Normally, I am not interested in doing this activity in the middle of the night when I should be sleeping.

But when I wake up because of restless legs syndrome or the Butterfly Thoughts that are extra needy or obnoxious, I wake up and organize Legos®. On average, I am ready to crawl back into bed within about thirty to forty minutes, and I am passed out before the night owls have even gone to bed.

The Rested Owl Is the Productive Owl

Speaking of night owls, I recently met with a client who is also a middle-aged woman, very successful, but who struggles with executive functioning, including time management. She and I have sometimes discussed her sleeping habits, and, frankly, they are really shitty. She doesn't get eight hours of sleep, or even close to it. She is a night owl and goes to bed normally between midnight and 1:00 a.m. However, her "bedtime" is inconsistent and largely depends on how much work she has.

Because she doesn't get a full night of sleep, she often needs to take a nap in the middle of the day.

In a recent discussion about her sleep, she said that she has always been this way. She remembers being in high school at a very intense preparatory school, where she prided herself on being able to pour a small cup of coffee and be ultra productive while the rest of her peers were resting.

And it worked for many years.

Until it didn't.

Now, in her mid-forties, she is recognizing that these habits are leading to poor time management challenges, decreasing her health, and ultimately causing a lot of issues in her work, her personal life, and her body. It is time for a change.

It is true that society favors the early bird, and candidly, I may appear a little biased, since this is my preference. But a night owl doesn't have to mean an unproductive owl, or an unhealthy owl, or a stressed-out owl.

Owls, in fact, sleep 10 – 12 hours per day unless something interrupts them.

Read that sentence again.

A night owl does not mean a no-sleep owl. In fact, owls sleep extensively, but they just do it during different hours than what humans are generally designed to do. So, my night owl reader, you may need to reframe your thinking about what it means to be a night owl. It may just mean that you fall asleep at midnight for your Perfectly Productive Bedtime Routine, and your Perfectly Productive Morning Routine doesn't start until 8:00 or 8:30 a.m.

If you do not have a career that supports a Perfectly Productive Workday starting at 10:00 a.m. (or later), then you may need to review your Perfectly Productive Day to fit into the puzzle and adjust your Perfectly Productive Bedtime Routine accordingly.

In other words, suppose you have to start work at 9:00 a.m., and perhaps that start time is a result of talking with your employer about adjusting it from the prior 8:30 a.m. request to something that is more aligned with your preference. You have determined, as a result of reading the Perfectly Productive Morning and the Perfectly Productive Sleep, that you need to fall asleep by 11:00 p.m. It is recommended that you start moving your bedtime back in increments until you reach 11:00 p.m. as your new bedtime. And now you will get the recommended eight hours of Perfectly Productive Sleep and have time in the morning to set yourself up for a Perfectly Productive Day.

When my sons were little, in fact, it even rings true today, we used to say that sleep begets sleep. The idea that their staying up and going to bed later meant that they would sleep in is completely crazy. The opposite would often happen. They'd go to bed late and be awake at 5:00 a.m. And then they would be little assholes later in the day when they were overly tired and didn't know how to manage their emotions.

Similarly, the idea that your lack of sleep leads to higher productivity, or that you adjust to not needing eight or more hours, is equally absurd.

You need sleep. Remember, we are all just little toddlers growing into adult bodies.

The label of Night Owl or Early Bird only relates to the time your body is ready to rise and shine and has nothing to do with the volume of sleep you got. So today, you are now a Night Owl who ensures her body is rested and ready to be the most alert you can be for the Tomorrow You.

When Today's Choices Meet Tomorrow's Energy

Sleep has become one of my biggest priorities and a non-negotiable part of my Perfectly Productive Day. In each section, I have included my fumbles and bloopers to show you that I am human, not perfect, and I don't live a Perfectly Productive Day every day.

I don't get a perfect night of sleep every night. There are nights when the watch records that I slept OK, Poorly, Compromised, or Very Poorly. And my body feels it – I can definitely tell when my watch records a poor night of sleep. More often than not, those poor sleep ratings can be directly tied to my other choices – usually involving alcohol or extra stress, but not always.

The in-the-moment me does not always make the best choices or consider the Tomorrow Me. I try to associate my actions with how I want to feel in the morning. When I don't want to be hungover or irritated that I did not sleep well or very well, then I decide to enjoy a non-alcoholic beverage or a cannabis-infused beverage instead.

Of course, that decision sometimes leads to sleep issues in a different form – waking up frequently because I have to pee a lot! Old lady problems, I guess…I know you also understand this.

So, here we are. We have finished your Perfectly Productive Day, and now we are finishing up your Perfectly Productive Sleep so you can wake up and live your Perfectly Productive Morning Routine – right back to the start of this book.

How do you feel?

At the end of the day, sleep is the reset button that allows us to show up again tomorrow. Some nights I hit that reset button cleanly, and other nights… well, not so much. What matters is noticing the patterns, forgiving the slip-ups, and making small changes that help the Tomorrow You wake up ready for what's ahead.

And that brings us full circle. The Perfectly Productive Day ends with rest, and begins again with the energy and clarity that only quality sleep can provide. You've now seen how each choice throughout your day—big or small—connects to the next. The question is:

How will you design your tomorrow?

Your Perfectly Productive Life

Like many journeys in life, you've made it this far, and you are probably already thinking about what comes next. We all do it. We hit a milestone, cross a finish line, or check a big box, and before we've even caught our breath, our minds are sprinting to the next race. It's a bit neurotic, isn't it? But it's also deeply human.

So, before we launch ourselves into the "what's next," let's do something we don't often give ourselves permission to do: pause and look back.

Let's check the rearview mirror for a moment.

Think about the small, consistent 1% changes you've experienced and experimented with while reading this book. Check your 1% Changes Checklist to remind yourself of the journey you've been on. What has changed?

Maybe you started drinking water before coffee.

Maybe you built in a five-second pause before scrolling on your phone.

Maybe you set out your workout clothes the night before or begin writing down your top priority at the end of each workday.

Maybe you stopped falling asleep with the TV blaring, or you started protecting the first thirty minutes of your morning as *your time.*

Individually, these things might have felt tiny. Almost insignificant. But together? They've started to shift your days in ways that matter. They've created momentum for living your Perfectly Productive Day.

If I could fold confetti into the spine of this book, this is the point at which it would come bursting out across your lap. You've earned a celebration (and I apologize for the imaginary mess.)

This life that you are living — this messy, beautiful, demanding, extraordinary life — is yours. You only get one. And here's the question: how will you take care of it?

How will you live it in a way that leaves you both productive and proud?

Because productivity, as you now know, is not simply about the number of boxes checked off or emails answered. Productivity is the byproduct of intentional living. It's the accumulation of micro-habits that align your day with your values, your goals, and your future self.

Looking Back: Your 1% Wins

Let's honor the work you've already done. It might not feel like much yet, but remember: this book was never about grand, sweeping transformations. It was about micro-shifts that build into something greater than the sum of their parts.

Think about the six categories of your day we've explored together:

- **Morning Routine**. You discovered the power of starting strong, whether through journaling, hydrating, stretching, or simply not letting your phone hijack your mind before you're even out of bed. You learned that mornings aren't about willpower; they're about systems you set up the night before.
- **Commute**. You reframed those in-between moments. Whether you're in traffic, on a train, or walking down the hall in your own house, commutes have become bookends: a chance to transition, reset, and choose how you arrive.
- **Workday**. You learned how to wrestle back control from distractions, how to design your hours with intention, and how to give yourself permission to focus deeply instead of glorifying multitasking.
- **Evening Routine**. You began closing loops, choosing reflection over chaos, and creating rituals that support your body and mind. Evenings became preparation, not leftovers.
- **Bedtime Routine**. You explored the gift of winding down with purpose, of honoring your tomorrow self by shutting down screens, setting intentions, and granting your body the rest it deserves.
- **Sleep**. You saw that sleep is not passive downtime, but active investment. It is restoration, memory consolidation, hormonal balance, and the foundation of every productive choice that follows.

Every chapter was designed with small, practical steps. Maybe you tried just one from each section. Maybe you latched onto one area more than another. That's okay. Progress is not about doing everything — it's about experiencing and experimenting, finding what fits, and stacking small wins.

This is the messy, beautiful truth of productivity: your progress doesn't show up in one dramatic leap. It sneaks in sideways. It builds gradually, like compound interest.

And today, as you look back, you'll see that you've already invested in yourself.

The Myth of Arrival

Here's something I want to make clear: there is no finish line.

I know, that's not always the most exciting thing to hear. We love checklists, certifications, medals, and markers that say, "You made it!" We long for that elusive day when the To-Do list is finally clear, the inbox is empty, and every system in our lives is running like clockwork.

But the truth? That day never comes. And that's not a failure — that's freedom.

Psychologists call this the *hedonic treadmill* – the tendency for people to quickly return to a baseline level of happiness despite positive or negative life changes — was first introduced by psychologists Philip Brickman and Donald Campbell in 1971. Each time we reach a new level of achievement or mastery, our brains quickly normalize it. The goalposts move. What once felt extraordinary becomes ordinary, and we start chasing the next extraordinary thing.

This is why people with immense wealth still want more. Why professionals who reach the top of their fields still feel restless. Why you, after reading this book and making dozens of changes, might still be asking:

"What's next?"

The answer is not to escape the treadmill. It's to get off autopilot. To stop sprinting blindly toward a finish line that doesn't exist and instead decide how you want to run.

Productivity is not about "arriving." It's about practicing. It's about choosing how you show up each day, again and again. It's about identity.

Productivity as Identity

Every time you make a 1% change — every time you choose water over mindless scrolling, or reflection over reaction — you are reinforcing a story about who you are.

You are telling yourself:

- *I am someone who takes my time seriously.*
- *I am someone who invests in myself.*
- *I am someone who can trust myself to make smart decisions and then follow through.*
- *I can rely on myself to be who I want to be more often than not.*

Over time, those stories become your reality.

This is the essence of self-perception theory. We don't just act because of who we think we are; we start to think we are the kind of person who acts that way. That's why identity matters.

You don't have to be the most disciplined, motivated, or organized person on earth. You just have to be someone who makes the small choice — today — to align with the identity you want.

And yes, there will still be bloopers. There will be nights when you binge a show past bedtime or mornings when you hit snooze three times. Those moments don't erase your progress; they're part of it. They are reminders that you are human and that the work of productivity is not about rigidity but resilience.

We've talked about my bloopers throughout this book because they matter. They matter not because they define us, but because they remind us that the messy moments are data – not failures.

Every time you stumble, you gain information.

- *Why didn't I follow through?*
- *What environment triggered me?*
- *What story was I telling myself?*
- *How can I design tomorrow differently?*
- *What is this event trying to tell me?*

This is why resilience is more important than perfection. Productivity isn't about flawless execution. It's about how quickly you bounce back. It's about the grace you extend to yourself and the lessons you extract.

The most productive people in the world are not the ones who never fall off track. They are the ones who get back on track the fastest, and they use tools and systems to do so – without any judgment.

Beyond the Day: The Ripple Effect

This book focused on a single day because our days seem manageable. Twenty-four hours is just enough time to feel and to hold in your hands. But the truth is that Perfectly Productive Days don't stop at midnight. They ripple outward.

- A week of productive days builds momentum.
- A month of productive days creates habits.
- A year of productive days reshapes your identity.
- A decade of productive days leaves a legacy.

What you've been practicing isn't just about "today." It's about building the life you want to look back on. It's about living in alignment with the Future You who thanks you for every small decision you made along the way.

Imagine yourself five years from now. What will your health look like if you continue prioritizing sleep? What will your career look like if you continue protecting your focus? What will your relationships look like if you continue carving out intentional time?

This is the compound interest of productivity.

Practical Next Steps

So, where do you go from here?

- **Revisit your 1% changes.** Make a list of the ten micro-shifts that felt most doable. Post them where you'll see them daily.
- **Schedule a quarterly reflection ritual.** Once every three months, look back on your progress. Celebrate wins, identify bloopers, and choose one or two new micro-shifts to experiment with.
- **Create a "Future You" practice.** Write a letter from yourself one year from today, thanking you for the choices you made. Keep it somewhere visible.
- **Share your Perfectly Productive Day Workbook.** Teach a family member, a friend, or a colleague one of the strategies from this book. Accountability and community will reinforce your own practice.
- **Stay curious.** Treat productivity like an experiment, not a verdict. Try new things. Discard what doesn't fit. Refine what does.

- **Continue the Growth Mindset.** Continue building a growth mindset by exploring the next book in *The Perfectly Productive* series.

Who you believe you are is who you are.

If you believe you are disorganized, scattered, or perpetually behind, you'll act in ways that reinforce that story. But if you believe you are productive — not perfectly, but consistently, intentionally, humanly productive — then you will keep making choices that align with that belief.

You have the tools, strategies, and frameworks. The DNA of your Perfectly Productive Day is in your hands. You are no longer striving to be productive; you are living it. That is no easy feat.

Don't stop choosing. The only way this stops working for you is if you stop working it.

Keep choosing to align your mornings with intention. Keep choosing to design your commutes so they transition you, not drain you. Keep choosing to focus, rest, protect your evenings, and honor your sleep.

Keep choosing to make 1% changes, even when they feel small.

Keep choosing to believe in your future self.

Because productivity is not about one perfect day. It's about a lifetime of choices that move you closer to the life you want to live.

Keep celebrating how far you've come. Stay curious about what's possible next. And, most importantly, give yourself permission to keep experimenting.

Your Perfectly Productive Day is not something to achieve once and for all. It's a practice. A mindset. A lifelong habit of choosing, again and again, the actions that bring you closer to the life you want to live.

So go ahead — step into tomorrow. Your Future Self is waiting, smiling, and cheering you on…and so am I. Thank you for taking this journey together with me. Now, go and live your Perfectly Productive Day.

ACKNOWLEDGMENTS

This book benefited from the guidance and support of many people who contributed in distinct and meaningful ways. I am especially grateful to Geo Derice, whose work as a coach, editor, and strategic guide (including the marketing) shaped this project from early concept through completion. His steady perspective, clarity, and commitment helped refine both the book's message and direction.

I am also deeply influenced by the work of productivity thought leaders and authors, including Cal Newport, David Allen, James Clear, Atul Gawande, and Mel Robbins. Their ideas and frameworks directly shaped the thinking behind this book and helped clarify how disciplined, intentional work can support a meaningful life.

On a personal level, I am endlessly grateful to my husband, Andy Tetlow, for his unwavering support and for never once complaining when I was gone for hours working on the book. To my sons, Keegan and Grayson, thank you for your patience, perspective, and for recognizing that "mom is the boss." You all encouraged me to take the 1% steps each week to ensure this project was completed. Remember our family motto of 2025: *There is always a solution.* I love you so much.

I am thankful to my mom and dad, Matthew and Victoria Mulder, for their constant encouragement and belief in me. Some of the childhood stories are ones that we still laugh about today. I haven't changed much…nor did I fall far from the tree. Thank you to my sister and her family for their support throughout the process. Zander, I am here to help you get your book published when you're ready.

I am also grateful to my writing partner, Sarah, for her collaboration, accountability, and steady encouragement. To my many friends who supported me along the way, some of which include Jessica, Kelly, Hayley, Jaime, Sarah, Shellie, and Gabby. Thank you for understanding when I had to cut my evenings short, for continually encouraging me to get to the finish line, and for grabbing your copy of the book!

Thank you to Jenna, whose Reiki session sparked the creative clarity that ultimately inspired this book, and to Michelle, my hypnotherapist, who helped me keep the creativity going.

My thanks also extend to my professional networking colleagues, including (but certainly not limited to) Belle Walker, Laura Doehle, Allison Tabor, Jessica Natkin, Margaret Abeles, Tony Q., the Dang Mastermind Group, and everyone in Provisors who offered encouragement and support along the way.

Finally, to everyone who supported this project by purchasing the book before it even launched, thank you for your trust in the outcome and belief in this work. Each contribution, whether practical, intellectual, or personal, played a role in bringing this book into the world.

NOTES

Introduction

[18] Carol Dweck, *Mindset*, 2006

[20] *Mel Robbins Podcast*, "#1 Neurosurgeon", Episode 227

Chapter 1

[34] *Mel Robbins Podcast*, "Motivation is Garbage," Episode 3

[40] *Mel Robbins Podcast*, "How to Get Motivated Even When You Don't Feel Like It," Episode 208

[42] *Mel Robbins Podcast*, "Simple Life Hacks That Will Change Your Future," Episode 217

Chapter 2

[45] Heijnen, S., Hommel, B., Kibele, A., & Colzato, L. S. (2016). Neuromodulation of Aerobic Exercise—A Review. Frontiers in Psychology, 6, 167146. https://doi.org/10.3389/fpsyg.2015.01890

[46] *Mel Robbins Podcast*, "Change Your Brain," Episode 218

[49] *Mel Robbins Podcast*, "Change Your Body," Episode 265

Chapter 3

[63] Napoleon Hill, *Think and Grow Rich*, 1937, p. 3

[64] Napoleon Hill, *Think and Grow Rich*, 1937, p. 5

64 Teresa Amabile and Steven Kramer, *The Progress Principle*, Harvard Business Review Press, 2011

Chapter 4

72 Katy Milkman, Julia Minson, and Kevin Volpp, "Holding the Hunger Games Hostage at the Gym," Management Science, 2014

Chapter 5

80 David Allen, *Getting Things Done*, Penguin, 2001

86 Norman Doidge, *The Brain That Changes Itself*, Penguin, 2007

86 Daniel Kahneman, *Thinking, Fast and Slow*, Farrar, Straus and Giroux, 2011

86 Charles Duhigg, *The Power of Habit*, Random House, 2012

86 Moruzzi, G., & Magoun, H. W., 1949. Brain stem reticular formation and activation.

Chapter 7

100 Roy F. Baumeister et al., "Ego Depletion: Is the Active Self a Limited Resource?" *Journal of Personality and Social Psychology*, 1998

100 Daniel Kahneman, *Thinking, Fast and Slow*, Farrar, Straus and Giroux, 2011

101 Cal Newport, *Deep Work*, Grand Central Publishing, 2016

Chapter 8

109 *Mel Robbins Podcast*, "How to Stop Procrastinating, According to the World's Leading Expert," Episode 12

115 Cal Newport, *Slow Productivity*, 2024, p. 60

Chapter 9

139 Michael Watkins, *The First 90 Days*, 2013, p. 229

140 Mueller, P. A., & Oppenheimer, D. M. (2014). *The Pen Is Mightier Than the Keyboard: Advantages of Longhand Over Laptop Note Taking. Psychological Science*, 25(6), 1159–1168

147 *Mel Robbins Podcast*, "How to Get Things Done, Stay Focused and Be More Productive," Episode 322

Chapter 11
159 Atul Gawande, *The Checklist Manifesto*, Metropolitan Books, 2009

Chapter 12
170 Eve Rodsky, *Fair Play*, Putnam, 2019

Chapter 13
181 Mihaly Csikszentmihalyi, *Flow*, 2008, p. 162-163
190 Cal Newport, *Digital Minimalism*, Portfolio, 2019, p.73

Chapter 14
200 Arthur C. Brooks, "The Lie We Tell Ourselves About Going to Bed Early," *The Atlantic*, June 10, 2021

Chapter 15
204 *Mel Robbins Podcast*, "Get Back on Track," Episode 270
207 *Mel Robbins Podcast*, "Get Back on Track," Episode 270
207 Arthur C. Brooks, "The Lie We Tell Ourselves About Going to Bed Early," *The Atlantic*, June 10, 2021

Chapter 16
211 Harvard Medical School, *Improving Sleep: A Guide to a Good Night's Rest*
214 *Mel Robbins Podcast*, "How to Get Better Sleep and Boost Your Learning, Memory, and Energy," Episode 116

Chapter 17

222 Harvard Medical School, *Improving Sleep: A Guide to a Good Night's Rest*, Table 2 on p.9

223 Arthur C. Brooks, "The Lie We Tell Ourselves About Going to Bed Early," *The Atlantic*, June 10, 2021

224 Napoleon Hill, Think and Grow Rich, 1937

Chapter 18

233 *Mel Robbins Podcast*, "The Real Reason Boys and Men Are Quietly Struggling & How to Support," Episode 317

234 E. J. Masicampo and Roy F. Baumeister, "Consider It Done! Plan Making Can Eliminate the Cognitive Effects of Unfulfilled Goals," 2011

234 Harvard Medical School, *Improving Sleep: A Guide to a Good Night's Rest*, p.14

Chapter 20

241 Harvard Medical School, *Improving Sleep: A Guide to a Good Night's Rest*, p.9

ABOUT THE AUTHOR

Sarah Tetlow's work is grounded in a simple conviction: productivity should support a full and intentional life, not compete with it. Over the course of more than two decades working inside high-pressure professional environments, including law firms, she witnessed how constant urgency, interruptions, and unexamined habits quietly drain focus, energy, and satisfaction, even among high-functioning, capable, and motivated professionals.

That firsthand experience shaped her philosophy and approach. Rather than teaching people to squeeze more into already-full days, Sarah helps high-achieving professionals design systems that reduce friction, protect attention, and make focused work possible in the midst of real life. Her work emphasizes intention over intensity and sustainability over short-term output.

Sarah is the creator of the ARTT® Email Productivity System, a practical framework designed to help professionals regain control of their inbox, reduce anxiety, and work with greater clarity. Informed by behavioral psychology and real-world application, her approach helps people replace reactive patterns with repeatable practices that support both performance and well-being.

A lifelong learner, Sarah is deeply committed to her own personal development and approaches each day with a growth mindset. She maintains intentional habits around reading, reflection, and focused work, believing that growth is built through small, consistent practices over time.

She lives with her husband and two sons in California. Sarah believes a truly productive day is one you can repeat without sacrificing what matters most.

RESOURCES

Your journey toward a perfectly productive
day does not stop at the last page.
When you visit the resources page, you will get access to:

• The 1% Daily Checklist covering every part of your day
• A preview of The Perfectly Productive Day Workbook
• The Firm Focus Vault with practical tools, trackers,
and templates to support your productivity

(Scan QR Code For Access To The TPPD Resources Page)
Start turning insight into action.